MW00799364

THE RUMBLE OF 1869

The Football Game That Started It All

Rutgers vs. Princeton
1869

ROBERT ILVENTO

THE RUMBLE OF 1869

Print ISBN: 978-1-09839-9-627
eBook ISBN: 978-1-09839-9-634

Thank you to the staff at Mudd Library in Princeton, the Alexander Library in New Brunswick, the Rugby School library in England and the Harvard Library in Boston for their detailed record keeping, thus archiving these great moments in history, to be stitched together for all to understand how the game of football evolved. Thank you to my many friends and family who read, edited and commented on both the novel and the screenplay. Your input was much appreciated and made it better and better. To the Rutgers, Princeton, Harvard, Yale and Rugby School programs, you are great examples of how these great games make ambitious teenage boys into better men.

We hope you enjoy,

THE RUMBLE OF 1869.

This book is dedicated to everyone who loves the game of Football, Soccer and Rugby.

We hope you enjoy,

THE RUMBLE OF 1869.

CHAPTER 1

IT WAS A COOL DAY IN RUGBY, ENGLAND, 1857. STEPHEN
Gano Sr. a husky red haired Scottishman stepped out of his humble, three-
room home, into the brisk, sunny day. Beside him stood his namesake,
Stephen Gano Jr. "How about a walk, Junior?"

Eager to spend time with the "legend," Stephen Jr. didn't need any
coercing. Heading toward town, the two strode purposefully onto the dirt
road in front of their home. His father greeted neighbors as they passed, but
all Junior wanted to do was talk about the upcoming football game.

"Ya know, Papa," said young Stephen, "Uncle Jack told me you know
you're gonna whoop a team, even before the match starts. How do you
know?"

Chuckling, Stephen Sr. replied, "Well Junior, when a team is weak I
can see it in their faces. Especially when they're young and eager bucks, I can
sense when they aren't ready to defeat us, when nerves will get the best of
'em. You need a strong will and strong spirit to win at football. "It's a game
that beats up your mind as well as your body."

Nearly giddy with excitement, Stephen Jr. hung on his father's every
word.

Stephen Sr. continued, "To captain a team, you have to be a good read
of mens strengths and weaknesses, not only of your own mates, but of your
opponents' too. You have to know where you're weak and vulnerable, where
you're not, whom you can use for brute strength, and who has the brains and
skills to work through the plays that require thought, timing and precision.

"Remember I told you, son, you have to have practiced strategies?"

Stephen Jr. nodded his head enthusiastically.

"When you have a smaller faster team, you want to play the kicking game" Stephen Sr. continued, "ya wanna keep the field big and the ball low and run the big boys back to the farm. If you're the bigger, taller team, you wanna play the running game, keep the field small, the ball high, and over-power them with your bulldozers or bulldogs. Ya also have to remember to watch the opposing players to see which ones have skills and which ones may lack endurance."

"So the leader has to choose 'stragedies' to help their squad win?" Stephen Jr. asked, mispronouncing the word strategies.

"Yes, Junior," Stephen Sr. encouraged. "Strategies are important, and so is the set up. As captain, I have to make sure I assign my mates accordingly. When the rules are being sorted out, you have to know your team well enough to know which ones will best help your mates win. Sometimes ya gotta tussel for 'em."

"Is that why Uncle Jack told me you're a football legend, Papa?" Stephen Jr. asked admiringly. Humbly, Stephen Sr. responded, "Aw, I'm no legend. I just play hard and try to bring honor to my family and folly to my friends."

"Ah, here we are," Stephen Sr. said, approaching the door to Richard Lindon & Company Leatherworks. Entering the building, they saw an assortment of animal pelts hanging from the ceiling, some still drying. All around, boots, shoes, and footballs were being made. The sights, smell and sounds mesmerized Stephen Jr.

With a handshake, Stephen Sr. greeted the owner, "Good morning Richard."

As Richard Lindon stopped to chat, a butcher with a blood-drenched apron walked past them. He was holding a burlap bag out of which a slimy, greenish, oblong pig bladder was dripping. He handed it off the leathersmith who would struggle to insert it into a hand stitched, four panel, leather casing.

Watching the pig bladder, Stephen Jr.'s eyes were wide and his mouth was half open. Richard Lindon affectionately asked, "And who is this fine young redhead lad?"

Refocusing, Stephen Jr. responded, "I'm Stephen Gano Jr. Stephen spelled with a ph. You can call me 'Junior.' It's my pleasure to make your acquaintance."

As he had seen his father do many times, Stephen Jr. reached out his hand. Meeting the lad's outstretched hand in a shake, Richard Lindon offered praise for Stephen Jr.'s excellent decorum and replied, "nice to meet you, Junior."

Stephen Sr. beamed with pride.

With a wink, Lindon queried, "What brings you in today Mr. Gano?"

William Gilbert, listening in, was visiting from the neighboring Gilbert Company, put down the box of leather laces he had come to borrow and joined the men. Stephen Sr. answered, "The Lumberjacks and the Coal miners face off at the Close, the playing field behind Rugby School, in two weeks. I'm here to order the game ball."

"And you're the captain yet again, eh?" Gilbert mused.

"Indeed I am, perhaps for one last time, gentlemen. That's if I don't let the wife have any say in the matter," Stephen Sr. conceded.

All eyes turned to watch the leathersmith insert the slimy green pig bladder into a four panel pigskin. It was an interesting process, necessitating that the employee tug and push and endure spurts of foul smelling fluids on their hands and face. After stuffing the bladder into the leather pig skin, the deflated ball was given to Mrs. Lindon, Richard Lindon's wife and mother to seventeen children. A distasteful job, Mrs. Lindon was somehow roped into the chore of blowing up the bladders in all the balls. Inserting a light orange clay pipe into the bladder's bloody neck, it took a huge amount of lung power to inflate. When finished, she carefully knotted the neck tightly and laced the ball closed.

Once completed, Richard Lindon quickly grabbed the ball from his wife and, gripping it tightly in one hand, raised it, brought his arm high and slightly back and threw, releasing the ball toward Stephen Jr.

Although surprised, Junior caught the ball with minimal effort. Smiling, Lindon commented, "You look like a footballer, just like your father. Now don't drop it; it's bad luck to drop the pigskin!"

"I know," Stephen Jr. acknowledged, "I won't drop it Mr. Lindon. My father taught me how to take care of the pigskin ball."

With great concentration, Junior threw the ball up in the air a few times. Each toss landed back in his hands safely. Reluctantly, he gave the ball back to Mr. Lindon.

Admiring the ball, sounding almost surprised, Richard Lindon stated, "There's been a greater demand for these balls lately. Not only are the boys at Rugby School playing more and more Rugby Football, but other boys and schools are ordering them too." I am working on a new India rubber insert to take the place of the bladder, and a brass hand pump to inflate it. That way we'll be able to make more consistent size balls of all shapes and sizes faster. Mrs. Lindon, looking on, "I can't wait for that".

William Gilbert chimed in, ``Ever since the Rugby school boys started playing William Ellis running style football in 1823, more and more balls have been made over the recent years. I think I'm making more footballs than shoes and boots these days!" Do you realize Junior that the Rugby school has been around since 1567. It's one of the oldest in England. One day Junior I hope I will see you playing there.

Addressing Stephen. Sr. Richard Lindon continued, "Come back Friday next and I'll have a game ball ready for you."

"Will do. Richard, William, good to see you both. See you again in a week. Thank you!" replied Stephen Sr. The Ganos shook the shop owners' hands and exited the building.

Stephen Jr. was beyond excited by what he had seen. As they walked toward the street, he was talking a mile a minute, "Wow, Papa, did you see how they make 'em? Did you see that bloody pig bladder going into the pigskin? I can't wait to see the new ball for the game! Will it look just like that one?"

"Yes, Junior," Stephen Sr. humored, "it was really interesting, and you got to be the first one to catch that ball! Our ball probably won't look just like that one. The size can be slightly different depending on what size bladder they get from the butcher. We'll just have to wait till next Friday to see what our ball looks like but it should be close to that size." These balls came a long way from the time the Roman soldiers used to kick around the severed heads of their fallen enemies for sport. Stephen Jr. looked at his father in disgust of what he just said.

It had been a grand adventure for young Stephen Gano Jr.

CHAPTER 2

TWO WEEKS LATER, ONE COULD SEE A SINGULAR, DETER-
mined focus in the faces of the crowd that moved along a dirt road through
the cool, dense air. They had one objective: get to the Close at the Rugby
School to see the game. The cloud of dust that accompanied their eager
footsteps could not diminish their enthusiasm.

On their way, the crowd passed the Gano home. Peering in the window
of the simple, wood shingled single story home, one could see a beautiful
blonde woman standing by the stove, cooking. Two young girls sat at the
table and a younger boy sat intermittently in a rocking chair by the fireplace.
The boy restlessly sat, then stood, flipping an oblong leather object in the air.
His eyes flashed toward the window, then to a clock on the wall.

"What time is it, Mum?" asked Stephen Gano Jr.

His mother, Jeanne Gano, shook her head as she once again answered
her energetic six-year-old son, "It's now 1:33 Stephen."

Impatiently Stephen Jr. urged, "Mum, we're gonna miss the first buck
if Uncle Jack doesn't hurry up!"

"If Uncle Jack told you he'd fetch ya, he will. He wouldn't promise
something he couldn't do," Jeanne replied.

With that a big, burly man burst through the wooden door. He carried
a bundle of long orange strips of cloth.

"Well, hurry along Stephen! We're going to miss the first buck if we
don't get moving," Uncle Jack boomed. "What's that there, Stephen ? Is that
the ball for the Rumble?"

Young Stephen shook his head "no" as he explained that it was one of
his father's winning game balls. The new ball is with my father. We picked it

up yesterday and it's a beauty. His mother helped him put on his jacket and tied a scarf around his neck. Within seconds, Stephen Jr. was running out the door. He pretended he was playing in a game, running back and forth, carrying the ball toward and avoiding imaginary tacklers and dodging their interference. He pitched the ball to his Uncle Jack as Jack lumbered out the door behind him.

"Pitch it back to me Uncle Jack," squealed young Stephen.

Stephen effortlessly caught the pass Jack threw. A true natural, Stephen Jr. proceeded to run excitedly in circles around his uncle.

Amused and laughing, Uncle Jack warned, "Don't drop it lad. Dropping the pigskin will bring you bad luck!"

As if he'd heard it a hundred times, Junior wearily responded, "I know Uncle Jack, I know."

More seriously, Jack queried, "So, you've been practicing?"

"Yep. I want to be a great footballer like you, Uncle Jack!" The child proudly stated.

"Well, I was a good footballer till I got this hitch in my step playing with the older bucks and their mates. Your father, though, he's a footballing legend! It sure would be a great honor to him and the family for you to become a great footballer too," encouraged Jack. Pausing for a moment, Jack added, "Ya know, most men would rather be a meater (coward) on the sidelines."

"Not me, Uncle Jack!" Stephen boasted. "Papa has been teaching me 'stragedies'."

"'Stragedies' eh? Well, you sure will need those," Jack said smiling.

Before long they arrived at the mostly dirt field where the game was to be played. Crowds filed onto the sidelines of the evergreen tree-lined field. The energy of the crowd was contagious as the eager spectators, some running, jockeyed for the best viewing spot.

As Uncle Jack and Stephen Jr. got closer to the field, they began to see tree branch wooden goalposts appearing through the dense afternoon fog.

Light rain began to fall as Jack and Stephen Jr. approached Stephen Gano Sr.. Gano Sr. a gregarious Adonis of a man, was greeting all that came in contact with him, till he greeted his brother and son. Standing together, the three peering across the field sized up the competition. The battle was about to begin.

After tying an orange cloth around his head, then around Stephen Jr.'s head, Jack handed the bundle to his older brother, who quickly handed one to each man on his squad. Some men arrived in proper daytime attire, most in their work attire all wearing shoes or boots. The rugged looking men were then busy taking off their top hats, overcoats and vests. Slowly, they tied the orange cloths around their heads, contemplating what was to come. Knowing suspenders could be easily grabbed, the men converted them into tight belts around their waist. They didn't want to give the other side any advantages.

The teams began the task of limbering up, stretching this way and that, making sure to ready every muscle for the ensuing battle. All the while, not one man took his eyes off the competition. Both squads were grunting and shouting encouragement, building their confidence and focus. Stephen Sr. rallied his team's enthusiasm, shouting out words of encouragement, "We're going to Batty-Fang 'em, my bricky lads!" and "Thrash them Coal miners" and "Shake a Flannin!"

More than 350 spectators crowded the boundaries, and more were coming. News quickly spread that a Rumble was about to begin. Continuing his efforts to incite spirited devotion, Stephen Sr. grabbed a short, bald headed man by the cheeks, got close to his bearded face, and queried, "Are we ready Mr. Oliver? I know you have it in ya. We need your best efforts, mate!"

Grinning, Mr. Oliver shouted, "Ready Captain Gano! We're all ready! Let's hammer the Coal miners!"

The Lumberjacks were ready for battle. A collective, angry, determined grimace marked the team. Excitement was in the air.

Meanwhile, Stephen Jr. was checking out the competition. He was feeling nervous as he looked at the forty or so men. Most were hard, weathered looking workingmen.

"Wow, look at the Coal miners, Uncle Jack!" he exclaimed worriedly.

Through his own eyes, looking at the same team, Jack saw nothing but a few tired old men and young, nervous lads. None, in his estimation, were prepared for the physical and mental war they were about to encounter.

"Not to fret, young Stephen. With your dad as their leader, the Lumberjacks have already won this match," Jack pronounced.

"But Uncle Jack, the game didn't even start yet. How could we have won?"

"Like you told me earlier, Jr., your dad has strategies."

"What 'stragedies' Uncle Jack?"

"Well, young Stephen," Jack began, "Ya see how your father is watching the other squad getting ready? He's noticing if they're arranged or not. He's seeing their nerves and sizing up the team in general. Are they taller, slower, faster or heavier than his team? Ya see, if it's a fast team, they'll be wantin' an immense field. Tall, big teams like to keep the ball high and bulldoze down the middle. It's all about figuring out what the other team's strengths and weaknesses are so he can plan accordingly."

Mesmerized by his uncle's words, young Stephen nodded. He watched as the Coal miners captain used his finger to draw their plan of attack in the cold hard dirt. Soon the rain would soften the dirt, rendering the field treacherous for the players. The team huddled around the captain trying to prevent their opponents from seeing their strategy.

Nonetheless, Stephen Sr. knelt and watched every move the Coal miners made. He knew their captain, Leo Doyle, from the occasions when they met at the town pub, "The Squirrel Inn." Leo was a tall, black haired, burly man. His salt and pepper beard was the only thing that betrayed his age.

Watching the captains on the field, Jack turned to young Stephen to comment, "Your father is observing their expressions and actions. He's noticing the guy wrapping a knee, the one stretching his back more than the others, the guy saying a prayer. Do you see the guy that's scared to death, Stephen?"

"Yes, Uncle Jack," Stephen responded, watching the Coal miners intently.

"Your dad can sense fear, Stephen. You have to have courage to be a great footballer. Courage is finding the strength to overcome your fears. You have to get past that fear and just play free," Jack instructed.

Enthusiastically, Stephen replied, "That's great, Uncle Jack! Mother wants me to be smart and father wants me to be fearless. I'm gonna be a good footballer alright!"

Beaming, Uncle Jack put his hand on young Stephen's shoulder and assured him, "You will be just that, Stephen! You will be just that!"

Moving slowly, Stephen Sr. casually approached the opposition. Leo smiled and offered his big hand in a formal greeting. "Hello Long Shanks," Leo teased, his Scottish brogue barely noticeable.

Gripping his hand firmly, Stephen Sr. replied, "Long time no see, Blacky."

"Loser buys pints at the Squirrel, eh?" Leo proposed.

Stephen Sr. nodded, "Yep, and I'm really thirsty!" But might go to the farmhouse barn this time considering the size of each team.

The men returned to their teams before the formalities of the game proceeded. With fervor, each delivered final encouragement to their players.

As was the custom, concerned family and friends made their way onto the field to offer their own last-minute advice, warnings and of course, wishes for bountiful luck. Using burlap sacks filled with falling chimney ash, young boys were marking the final boundaries on the enormous 200 feet wide by 400 feet long mostly dirt playing field.

Finally, the captains walked mid-field and ceremoniously greeted one another with a vigorous handshake. Before the first buck (kickoff), they discussed the final rules of play.

Captain of the Coal miners, Leo Doyle, queried, "How many men do ya hov?" His brogue was clearly evident.

"About forty," Stephen Sr. answered. "What about you?"

"Aboot the same," came the response.

"Too many mates for running with the ball. Fair catch free kick rule? That would be easier for us both. Yea or Nay?" asked Stephen Sr.

"Yea then. Me mates enjoy the free kicks," Leo agreed.

"Match is to five or six goals. Under, over, or both?" asked Stephen Sr.

"Since we hov forty a side, first squad to scair five'll take the egg. Over or under is good with me. Some of me guys doon git around like they used to," Leo admitted.

Leo looking back at his team, he noted the out of shape older players. They were tough, though, and he knew they'd rise to the occasion.

A kick over or under is allowed fer a goal, or ya ken push it over the line. No running with the ball in this one. Leo confirmed as he nodded to a nearby man, signaling for him to put the ropes across the goal posts. The scoring team will have the choice to buck again or not.

"Agreed then," Stephen nodded, "Now, who's your referee?"

Turning toward the crowd, Leo yelled, "I choose James Odurn." A short, chubby fellow, James had played many a Rumble, until his injury. He knew the game as well as anyone.

Following suit, Stephen Sr. yelled into the crowd, "I choose Frank Taylor." Frank was a giant of a man with a black patch over his left eye. He too, had played in his share of Rumbles.

The men stepped out of the crowd to join the two captains mid-field. Handshakes were exchanged. Each referee took a white handkerchief out of his front pocket and tied a knot in one end. Then they returned the knotted handkerchiefs to their pockets.

Leo addressed Frank Taylor, "Toss the coin fer first buck?"

As if he'd done it a thousand times, Frank Taylor stated, "I'll toss it twice. The first toss will be for first buck, the second for defense goal. Gano, you make the call."

With that, Frank reached into his pocket and pulled out a large silver coin. He showed the captains that there was no trickery. Indeed, the coin had two different sides, one heads and the other tails. He flipped it high into the air, letting it hit the ground bouncing.

"Heads are called, " Stephen Sr. declared.

The coin landed tails.

"Tails it is," announced Frank Taylor. "The Coal miners will get the first buck." Leo agreed.

Laughing out loud, Leo shouted to his team, "Oh, the luck of the Scottish is upon us already!"

Stephen Sr. cut through the shared laughter to insert, "Oh, it won't last long."

"Make the call," Frank Taylor commanded, as he prepared to toss the coin a second time.

Leo shouted, "Tails," as the coin went up again.

"Tails it is," Frank declared.

Jubilant over his good fortune, Leo quickly put his finger up in the air, testing for wind direction. Pointing into the wind, Leo announced, "We will defend that goal to begin."

With the coin toss complete, the eighty or so men joined their respective captains' midfield. Stephen Gano Sr. offered the prayer. As he bowed his head, the players and spectators did the same. No one uttered a sound as Gano prayed, with Stephen Jr. following his fathers every move.

"Please Lord, bless our bodies and our souls in this war, this friendly war, a war not fought with guns or swords but with bodies and brains. Bless all these men and return them to their families unscathed by the charitable brutality that will shortly come upon us all. Amen."

A communal "Amen" swept the area.

Once again, the captains shook hands before heading to their appointed sides with their teams. Gano Sr. returned to his mates sporting a devilish grin. They were eager to start.

The referees were the first to move to their locations. Organizing themselves into their assigned positions, half of the Lumberjacks walked out to the middle of the field. They were the "bulldozers," the men who would push their way through the opponents as they struggled to move the ball down the middle of the field to make a goal. They would attempt the tried and true, brutal "wedge play," in which teammates would interlock arms and ram their way through the blockers. The ball handler would follow behind, kicking and dribbling the ball on the ground. Running with the ball was prohibited in this match..

The "fielders" made their way to the edges of the field. They would wait for the ball to come loose from the middle skirmish, or for the captain to call a set play using hand signals. That meant they had an opportunity to quickly kick and or bat the ball down the field in an attempt to score. The best kickers were the captains of the enemy's goal stationed in front of the opponents' goal. Not to be confused with the team captain, the goal captains would stand close to their opponent's goal line in the hopes of a quick steal and score.

On the field, the Coal miners organized themselves similarly.

Once the players were in their spots, the captains relayed the rules they had agreed upon. Yelling, Leo listed, "No runnin' wit the pigskin mates! Kick it over or under or push it over. Fair catch and free kick are permitted. Be ready... Gano wants to hammer us quickly, lads!"

There were few rules prohibiting violence in a Rumble. The games were violent and often ended with serious injuries. A tough bunch, filled with piss and vinegar, the Coal miners were nonetheless feeling a bit intimidated. Nervously, they stared down the Lumberjacks. They were determined to beat the legendary Stephen Gano Sr. and his team.

Shouting to his mates, Gano Sr. was eager to thrash his opponents, yelling "All ready for first buck ?"

With a roar, they responded, "Ready, captain!" It began to rain harder.

They looked eagerly to one another, waiting for the signal that the game could begin. Frank Taylor held one arm in the air as a signal of readiness. He then dropped his arm and the game began.

The Coal miners' captain used his boot heel to pound a kicking tee into the rain softened earth and placed the oblong ball onto the tee. Backing up, with singular determination, Doyle ran toward the ball, kicking it with all his might in the direction of the Lumberjacks' goal. Stopping the ball on a crazy bounce, his teammate began to kick the ball forward, but the Lumberjacks quickly took it away, gaining control.

Captain Gano gave hand signals overhead. Like a well-choreographed ballet, with the ball in the air, another Lumberjack player waved his hand, signaling his intention to fair catch and free kick. Executed perfectly, the fair catch was followed by a boot heel tee free kick. Moving the ball across the field, one Lumberjack player kicked to another, who quickly kicked to a running player stationed in front of the goal. Seamlessly, the ball was kicked and went over the outstretched hands of the defenders and over the cross string. The first goal of the game was scored.

Lumberjacks 1: Coal Miners 0

Brutal and bloody, the game was fraught with pushing, grabbing, elbowing, tripping, huffing, puffing and blocking. The physical and emotional challenges were unrivaled, only made worse by the steady, sometimes heavy rain. Sloshing and sliding the players used their hands and arms, legs and torsos, and even their heads to move, push, and bat the ball to their opponent's goal line. With bodies slamming, hacking of the shins and horse collar plays being the most brutal way to disband a player from the ball, the game was brutal in every way.

Since the Lumberjacks scored, they began with a short buck. It was time for a flying wedge play and with interlocking arms, the gathering bulldozers had only one thing in mind: mow down anything between them and the goal. Pushing down the center of the field, the human wedge, running five shoulders wide with interlocking arms, crushed anyone that got in their way. Muddied and bloodied, as they moved, human carnage was made manifest. Broken fingers and noses, bruised hips and knees, smashed and oozing bloody heads and arms were just the beginning. Two men were dragged off the muddy drenched field, barely conscious.

Angry and determined, the Lumberjacks didn't stop. Along with their captain, they reached the goal and pushed another over.

Lumberjacks 2: Coal Miners 0

Stephen Sr. observed the carnage. Passing an opponent with an obvious broken nose, one of Stephen's teammates commented, "you should get attention on that."

The man groaned, "No substitutions," indicating he'd be staying in the game.

With sympathy and heartfelt understanding, another player shook his head as he walked by. Motivated by their teammate's bravery, the Coal miners fought their way down the field with a similar wedge play to push one over themselves to score a goal.

Lumberjacks 2: Coal Miners 1

Despite starting with the buck, the Coal miners couldn't prevent the Lumberjacks from stealing the ball almost immediately. Bigger, faster, and smarter, the Lumberjacks were destroying the Coal miners. With continued hand signals, Gano gave commands for a series of fair catches, free kicks, and bulldozing plays. They scored again.

Lumberjacks 3: Coal Miners 1

The Lumberjacks kicked the ball short but high in the air. A Lumberjack was ready and eager to receive it. Waving his hands over his head, he was signaling that he had the ball in his sights, ripe for a fair catch. What he didn't see was the Coal miner who was determined to stop him. Leading with his shoulder, the fast-running Coal miner slammed into the unprotected Lumberjack, rendering him unconscious.

The giant referee Frank Taylor threw a white penalty flag way up in the air for the first penalty of the game. The referee awarded a free kick to the Lumberjacks. The Coal miners were required to move ten paces away from the ball. Stephen Sr. giving hand signals for a set play, ran hard to the ball, made a long kick to a running teammate who called a fair catch and quickly put one through the uprights, straight, and over the cross string.

Lumberjacks 4: Coal Miners 1

Both sides suffered many injuries as the brutal game progressed. The rain intensified, further muddying the terrain and endangering the players. Reduced in numbers, hitting and sliding, the game became more and more precarious, and the violence increased as the Coal miners and Lumberjacks duked it out.

Shouting angrily, Leo Doyle tried to fire up his players. His brogue got stronger, "Keep your heed! Don let 'em gie tew ya! Gie the baw and smash em!"

Surveying his men, Doyle continued, "Look to James Fitter! (James was the biggest man on the Coal miners team). James, heet that widge heed on! We've got to burst up their widges! We must gie that baw out. They geet fur goals. We need to kitch up now! We need tae scair, NOOOW!"

Having heard his name, James was humbled and questioned, "Who me?"

"Aye, ye!" Leo praised.

James gathered his courage and declared, "I'll hit 'em low. I'll hit 'em at the bootstraps. I'll get 'em at their knees. I'm gonna drop those bulldozers."

Shaking his head in agreement Leo followed, "Reedy lads? Let's gie 'at pigskin!"

The Lumberjacks got the ball after the Coal miners buck. Once again, the Lumberjacks called upon their strength and precision, locking arms to form another wedge. James was determined not to let them score. Crashing low into the moving muddy maul, James knocked players aside as if they were toys and the Coal miners did indeed take control of the ball.

With a mini wedge of three players, the Coal miners turned toward the Lumberjacks goalpost and marched down the field with relative ease. Pushing threw another score !

Lumberjacks 4: Coal Miners 2

The crowd went crazy.

"That away lads!" Leo shouted. "Now we're playin' the Coal miners' gam! Let's make this buck coont, men! Bulldozers, let's ram it doon, win the scrum, and then ram it doon agin!"

In contrast, Gano shouted, "Ok Lumberjacks...we've let the Coal miners back into the match...we have to stop 'em from taking another goal. We have to take the egg! Get that ball before they get a wedge set!"

Bloody and exhausted, Leo etched another tee into the mud with his boot heel. He placed the ball and signaled for James to go far right. James burst down the field to haul in Leo's kick. Calling for a free catch, he caught the ball and quickly kicked one over for a goal.

Lumberjacks 4: Coal Miners 3

Gano coached a team member, "Alexander, after the buck, scurry in there and get that football! Then kick it to me. Let's pull this off and end this now!"

"Will do, captain," Alexander obliged, confident he could outrun the tired Coal miners.

Having made the previous goal, the Coal miners started with the buck again. Lacking precision, the ball was kicked but no one made immediate contact with it. As promised, Alexander pursued it with a vengeance.

Once in his possession, with admirable precision, Alexander was able to accurately kick it to Gano who controlled it like it was a well-trained dog. Moving the ball down the field unchallenged, Gano effortlessly kicked the ball high and long. Despite the many goalkeepers' efforts, the ball sailed above their reach and over the cross string.

Lumberjacks 5: Coal Miners 3, Match over.

The muddied Lumberjacks immediately surrounded their captain in frenzied jubilation. In the pouring rain, congratulations flowed easily as the thirty or so remaining players celebrated the win. After the obligatory hugs, handshakes and congratulations the thirty or so Coal miners walked off the field, heads hung low.

Later that evening, cleaned up, banged up, bruised and bandaged, both teams gathered at a large red farmhouse barn. The rain had subsided and a "kegger" was about to begin. Arriving with food and beverage, players walked and limped in with their wives, girlfriends, and children. Looking around one might have mistaken the barn for an infirmary.

Standing on a stump, Leo called his men to join him as he began his speech. Hoots and hollers could be heard throughout the barn.

"Please, gie us yer attention," called the captain. Once silence reigned, he continued, "It was a greet gam today. The legend, Stephen Gano, en his

Lumberjacks are true champions. We got beat up, but not beat down. Hauld yer heed high and let's toast to the victors!"

Everyone raised a glass.

"It is mah preevilege to gie to the victors this pigskin from today's gam."

Leo held the dirty, beat up game ball high in the air as cheers ensued. Having wrenched his knee late in the game, Stephen Gano Sr. walked with a little hitch toward the stump. Stepping off the stump, Leo shook Stephen's hand and then ceremoniously presented him with the ball holding it up high into the air.

Gano stepped onto the tree stump to offer some words. "It was a brilliant match of skill and guts," he began. "With the first buck going our way, we gained an edge that led us to overcome you Coal miners today. You miners never gave up though. Frankly, we Lumberjacks were fortunate to come out alive. Luck had the muddy pigskin bounce our way more times than not."

After a pause, Gano continued, "Thank you to the Coal miners for your guts, glory, and praise."

Holding the ball over his head, Gano gave praise to one exemplary teammate. "Above all others," he went on, "one player stands out. This ball goes to a Lumberjack who merits credit above all others. That mate is.... Jimmy Doyle. Jimmys' fine kicking and wedge cracking were pivotal to winning our game today. Without James, we certainly would not have prevailed."

Great applause rose as Jimmy made his way to Gano. The two men shook hands as Gano handed off the ball. Nearby, Jimmys' girlfriend watched adoringly.

Stepping onto the stump, Jimmy offered a few words, "Thank you for the kind words, captain! I accept this ball for the Lumberjacks, a team of one will, with a great leader!"

Hoots, hollers, and applause once again swept the barn, as congratulatory hugs and handshakes were offered. Releasing the ball, Jimmy passed it into the crowd to be admired and signed with an inkwell pen that was handed out by a player's wife. It was tradition to collect all participants' signatures on the game ball.

A bountiful supper followed, complete with music and song, dancing and fanciful storytelling. Ample beef, game birds, ale, cigars and whiskey circulated as well. Obvious to all in attendance were the players who were there with their bruises and injuries that were visible to all.

CHAPTER 3

TEN YEARS HAD PASSED SINCE "THE RUMBLE" BETWEEN THE Lumberjacks and the Coal miners football game. At the Squirrel Inn Stephen Gano Jr. was enjoying a lemonade and his father an ale. Despite his mother's admonitions, Stephen Jr. had established himself as an accomplished footballer at the Rugby School, with a reputation for winning. He was walking in his father's footsteps and proud of it.

Drinking a little too much ale, some of the men at the Squirrel Inn were becoming rowdy. A man from the village of Clifton noticed a beautiful, red-haired girl across the room. Having consumed way too many ales himself, his rudeness ran unchecked. He decided to taunt the bruiser from Newbold with whom she sat.

"You should have better taste than that," the Clifton man scoffed, addressing the beautiful girl. "Why would you choose to be with that ruffian?" He spat on the floor, emphasizing his disdain.

The "bruiser" was not about to take the insult quietly. On his feet in seconds, a scuffle began. Before any punches could be thrown, however, friends of both men jumped in to stop the fight. Separated, the men continued shouting and cursing, flailing and struggling. In the midst of their aggression, a suggestion spewed forth: why don't we settle this with a Rumble.

"Yeah, we'll shettle it with a commun-ity game!" shouted the drunken Clifton man. Puffing out his chest, he continued, "We'll shee what shide of town haz better men!"

Also fully inebriated, the Newbold man slurred, "in lieu of further alter-cashun, with an ecshellent excush to play another game," his pronouncement was paused while he belched wildly, "the proud village of Newbold challenges the equally proud village of Clifton to a com-mu-ni-ty football game. We'll show you who's got better men!"

The crowd broke out in boisterous hoots and hollers.

"Sho," slurred the Newbold man, "Are we then in favor of such a match?"

"Aye in favor," came a chorus of voices, "aye!"

Above the din of "ayes" could be heard female voices in a definitive sound of, "NOOOOOOOOOOO!"

A man from Newbold shouted, "It is agreed then!"

In a more formal statement, someone announced, "In this year of 1867, "The Rumble" between Newbold and Clifton will take place at the Close field on the first Saturday of December, at three o'clock in the afternoon, after the first shift. Rules will be determined by captains once they are chosen."

With bumping mugs, pint glasses raised and shots of whiskey downed enthusiasm for the next game swept the room. Though he hadn't played in years, all eyes turned to Stephen Gano Sr. once again. Clifton residents sought his wise leadership. Aware of the attention, Stephen Sr. wondered if he had another Rumble in him.

CHAPTER 4

JEANNE GANO STOOD OVER THE COUNTER, DUTIFULLY MIX-
ing biscuit batter. Her husband stood behind her, affectionately rubbing her
shoulders, fully aware of her disapproval. The Gano siblings sat at the table,
Stephen Jr. holding a ball he had gotten at school. Awaiting "The Rumble,"
there was a lot of nervous energy.

Addressing her husband, Jeanne demanded, "Make this your last
Rumble!"

"Don't worry, Jeanne, I can still hold my own with those young bucks,"
Stephen replied.

"Town gossip says you'll allow carrying the ball in this game," Jeanne
accused.

"We'll only allow carry if the squads are at fifteen a piece as agreed,"
Stephen Sr. defended. "It's a wide open field with only fifteen players."

"Who are 'we'?" Jeanne asked.

"The Captains," Stephen replied.

"Oh, you mean YOU," Jeanne taunted. "You know carrying the ball
makes for an even more brutal contest. Don't come howling at me if you
break a tooth or worse, God forbid. Your younger brother, Jack, almost
lost his legs from a running Rumble. As it is he got that hitch for the rest
of his life. You're lucky you haven't been injured, Stephen. I'd like to keep
it that way!"

Chuckling, Stephen Sr. tried to assuage his wife's concerns, "That's why
the young bucks shouldn't Rumble with the old bucks. Plus, I'd rather lose a
tooth than lose to Newbold."

Stephen Jr. was practicing moves, playfully wrapping his arm around his dad's waist in a pretend tackle. Still believing he could teach his son a thing or two,

Stephen Sr. advised, "Always keep your eyes to the sky when you're striking or tackling, Junior. Otherwise you can lose your legs." His dad had preached about that "head up" move for years, and Stephen Jr. faithfully practiced, both on and off the field.

Shaking her head, Jeanne snickered, "Dumb bucks, putting their chest development ahead of their brain development." I won't watch another Rumble.

Jeanne looked at her son and said, "Stephen, you are a smart young man. All these years, Uncle Peter has paid for you to go to Rugby School. You should be thinking about college now. Going to that preparatory school gave you a great advantage. You got a good education and you worked hard enough to get accepted to all of those colonial colleges in the United States, your Uncle offered to pay all your debts associated with college. That's what your thoughts should be about, not rumbling with the other old dumb bucks. Do you understand?"

Listening to every word his mother said, young Stephen sighed and answered, "I understand mother." After a pause, he asked, "How do you think Newbold's team will play us today Papa ?"

Exasperated, with a nervous chuckle, Jeanne observed, "You're just like your father!" Looking from father to son she stated, "Men have been playing with their balls since their existence! Far be it from me to try to change that now!"

Amused by her own statement, Jeanne looked at her husband and smiled. He reluctantly smiled back, knowing Jeanne was right.

"Listen Stephen," Jeanne added, "Your studies must be paramount. Always remember, an education will give you the opportunity to make a good life for yourself. By using your brains instead of your body, the world will be open to you. Look what going to Harvard did for your Uncle Peter. Set your sights on going to college in the states, and you will do well."

"They do play football in the states, right?" queried young Stephen.

Shaking her head and smirking, Jeanne responded, "Well, you'll find out, won't you?" Then she added somberly, "Remember Stephen, when you make your fortune, always take care of your sisters. Your older sister, Morgan, will especially need your help. People often treat animals better than they treat people like her."

"I know, mother," Stephen Jr. replied. His youth belied his wisdom. "I've seen how some people act towards Morgan. I'll always be her big brother, even though she is my older sister. I understand her, and I understand what she needs."

"Stephen, you're a special person. Most people don't even try to understand anything about your sister's peculiarities," Jeanne said, shaking her head in frustration.

Sharing his mother's discouragement, Stephen Jr. shook his head in agreement. Then asked, "Mum? If you're so keen on education, how come we aren't rich like Uncle Peter?

"Well Stephen," Jeanne reflected, "financial riches aren't the only kind of riches. Our family is rich with honor, happiness and respect from the community. We are rich in family, love, and kindness."

"Those are things money can't buy, Junior," But you can have both Stephen Sr. chimed in.

Connected in love, gratitude, and pride, Morgan and Carly Ann joined their parents and Stephen Jr. for a family hug in the middle of the kitchen. While hugging, Jeanne further impressed, "It will offer you the promise of a bigger and better life!"

Teasing his wife, Stephen Sr. offered, "Thank the good Lord for my brother's fine brain and financial success." I had the brawn. Jr. you have both, don't take it for granted.

With utmost solemnity, Jeanne Gano looked her husband in the eye and pleaded, "Stephen, please, make this your last Rumble!"

Returning her gaze, Stephen told his wife, "I love you and the kids very much. My knees and back have been aching lately. I promise, this will be my last Rumble."

Stephen Sr. kissed his wife on the lips, and then kissed each of his daughters on the forehead. He nodded at his son and together they walked out the door. Stephen Sr. turned briefly and made eye contact with his wife. The Rumble was waiting on their attendance.

"So what are the strategies, Pa?" Junior asked his dad on the way.

"Well, I was thinking," Stephen Sr. began, "a few on the Newbold squad will have played with me in the past, so they might anticipate my tried and true strategies. We have to try to surprise them. I'm thinking about putting in some 'William Ellis of your Rugby school fame style, razzle dazzle 1823 running plays with lots of laterals. Your speed on the outside after the final toss will be too much for them, son. It'll be different than most Rumbles. In this match, we're only playing with fifteen men on each side."

"For sure I'll outrun them. And wow, Pa," Stephen Jr. exclaimed. "Only fifteen a side? How'd you make that happen for a community game?"

"Only the best men from each village are allowed to step up for this one. The other captain and I agreed to turn away the newcomers and the worn out. Not sure how I got roped into this one," Stephen Sr. said with a sly smile. "We have the gigantic Kenny Ford on our team. Jack Rabbit Jimmy Jones, too. He's fast! We have a good combination of size, speed, and spirit. And we've got you!"

"Giant Kenny Ford," Stephen Jr. repeated. "How big is he again?"

"Near seven feet, 400 pounds," Stephen Sr. confirmed. "He's a true thrasher and a great intimidator of all God-fearing men."

"Wow, yeah," Stephen Jr. exclaimed, "they'll be really surprised when they see that coming at 'em!"

"That's the whole idea, Junior," his dad reminded. "Surprise is a big part of footballing strategies. That's also where the thinking comes in. We want the other team to have to consider what to do next. While they try to sort us out, we want to be putting one over on 'em or be running the ball to the goal. While they stare at Kenny coming at them, you'll blaze around the end and he will get you the ball as they try to tackle him. We'll use a lot of head fakes and laterals when we need 'em. But don't kid yourself, they're gonna be fierce and the game brutal!"

"Pa, what will the other rules will be this time?" Stephen Jr. asked, starting to play the game in his head.

"We won't know 'til their mugs are in our line of sight. Then their captain and me, we'll decide on the final rules of play," Stephen Sr. answered.

CHAPTER 5

WHEN THE GANOS ARRIVED AT THE FIELD, EAGER YOUNG
boys with sacks of gray chimney dust were marking the boundaries of play.
It was cold and overcast, but that didn't deter the large crowds, a mix of old
and young, women and men rich and poor from gathering. They brought
food, drink, and cigars, the smells lingering in the dense air. Bagpipes played
in the distance.

True to expectation, only the best men were arriving at the Rumble
and it showed. Captains and players alike were sizing up each arrival. As
familiar players stepped forth, a flurry of whispers ensued. Every man looked
confident, capable, and willing. Players stripped off their overcoats, vests, and
top hats, and proceeded to tie their team's colored cloth around their heads
readying the men for battle. The Clifton squad donned orange and Newbold
donned green. Start time was three o'clock.

Leaning close to talk to his son, Stephen Sr. firmly instructed, "Stay
alert, Junior." Then he asked, "Do you see Uncle Jack?"

Looking around, Stephen Jr. replied, "I don't see him yet, but I know
he'll be here!"

Moments later, Jack rushed onto the field. As he eyeballed the Newbold
team, he knew it would be a battle requiring great courage and stamina.

Spotting Jack, Stephen Jr. waved his hands and shouted, "Come on
Uncle Jack! It's almost time for the first buck!"

Joining his brother and nephew, Jack observed, "This will be a great
contest!" With concern in his voice and on his face, Jack questioned, "Are
we ready, Stephen?"

Stephen Sr. responded, "We're ready, but they're ready too. Some of their players played for the Lumberjacks way back when. They have a squad I'd be proud to captain."

Jack coached, "You'll just have to have superior strategies. Run Kenny Ford to tire them out. It will be tough to bring the big man down, so that's an advantage you have. And young Stephen here, he's proven himself to be an excellent runner. Pitch to him as often as needed."

"Yeah, with Ford running, we'll keep it on the ground. Hopefully they'll tire from tackling the giant. Then we'll get the ball to our kickers or to Junior. They'll run toward the goal and maximize the score attempts. I've been talking to Junior about using his speed. So that will be our strategy," Stephen Sr. agreed.

Jack warned, "It will be a brutal game, Stephen!"

Staring down the opposition, Stephen Sr. nodded his head in agreement. Seeing a bunch of battle tested men on the other side, many who he had captained in the past.

As each team limbered up, they glared at their opponents. As before, each was determining where the weakest links were and of whom they had to be most careful. They looked for strong emotions, be they nerves or arrogance. Every detail informed a better game plan.

Signaling the game was about to begin, the captains walked to center field, greeting each other with a strong vigorous handshake.

Joseph Griggs, captain for the Newbold team began, "As agreed previously, we will play fifteen on fifteen. Ball over only, unless run through. Running is allowed. No fair catch or free kick. The three-punch rule will be honored before a player gets disqualified. Anyone found wearing a metal plate under his clothes will be immediately disqualified. The match will end with the first squad to score five goals."

Captain of the Clifton squad, Stephen Sr. nodded, saying, "Do you agree with the chosen referees?"

Looking at the two refs standing on the sidelines, Joseph nodded, "Yes, I agree with these referees, Stephen."

Dutifully, Stephen Sr. signaled for the referees to join him and Joseph at center field while shouting, "Bring 'em over for the coin toss." The captains convey the rules to the referees. The coin is tossed twice.

The coin toss resulted in Clifton winning first buck and Newbold winning choice of goals. Pointing into the wind, Joseph motioned to his men which goal was theirs to defend first. With the goal decision made, the men from both teams circled the field, knelt, and bowed their heads in prayer.

Once again, Stephen Sr. led the prayer for the players: All the players on both teams locked arms in solidarity.

I find myself once again, dear Lord, asking for your blessing as we tempt fate and face imminent brutality. These proud villages of Clifton and Newbold are about to battle for the bully football, pitting our communities' grit, courage, spirit, and strength of mind against one another. We pray that you give us courage, keep us safe, and allow each of our mates to return to our families and friends unscathed from the certain brutality that will fall upon us all.

Amen

An echo circulated as the men repeated, "Amen."

Boisterously, the teams separated onto the field, both squads configured in similar fashion. The teams were well organized, eager, and appeared to be equal in talent.

"Take your positions, mates," Stephen Sr. yelled.

The players readied in their positions. Having won first buck, Stephen Sr. kicked the ball far towards the enemies goal to a Clifton fielder. He then picked it up and lateralled it to Big Kenny Ford who ran just beyond a wedge of blockers. After a vicious tackle by five defenders, he threw the ball straight into the air. One of the attackers was slow to rise. The game had begun.

With the ball in the air, both squads fought to gain possession. Using arms, legs, hands and heads, the ball was batted back and forth. Each of the well-matched teams hoped for a run attempt or a kick. Bouncing, pushing, tackling and running, the teams brutally volleyed back and forth. Finally, Stephen Sr. skillfully seized the ball and ran, avoiding the tacklers. With the help of the flying wedge in front of him, the captain of the Clifton team expertly made his way to the goal. The Newbold team chased, but Stephen Sr. ran the first goal over. The refs each raised two arms, signaling a score.

Clifton 1: Newbold 0

As if in slow motion, the gruesome battle was hard to watch, but no one could look away. The speed of the game wore the players down and the contact became more ferocious with each play. Filled with unprecedented brutality, with every body slam and violent tackle the onlookers knew it would only get worse.

Scoring the first goal stimulated adrenaline. The Clifton team was determined. They shouted out accolades to their leader for the goal he had scored.

"Let's keep on 'em mates!" Stephen Sr. encouraged. "Get the buck and bulldoze to the goal. Let's end this contest early!"

As their captain offered hand signals, the team was ready to attack. In a synchronized effort, they surrounded the next buck, moving the ball down the center of the field. With giant Kenny Ford at the front of the wedge, they viciously destroyed ambitious tacklers with every advance, then ran another score across.

Clifton 2: Newbold 0

There were few rules prohibiting hacking, tripping, pushing or pile driving. Each time a goal was scored, possession switched, the game became more cruel. Using whatever body parts were convenient, the men moved the ball toward the enemy's goal. After a lengthy battle of back and forth, another ball was finally kicked over the string lined goal posts by the Clifton team.

Clifton 3: Newbold 0

Captain Gano continued to guide his team with hand signals. Lateral strategies were used as the fastest of Clifton's players including Stephen Jr. tired out the Newbold team. Stephen Jr. got the ball at the end of another brutal wedge play. He scored easily receiving a lateral toss as the runner was being tackled he crossed the goal again.

Clifton 4: Newbold 0

With each score, spectators dragged any injured players off the field.

As the game began to look like a landslide, Joseph, the Newbold captain, shouted, "We have to stem this tide. We must halt Clifton. Let's break up their flying wedge. Let's go men, let's score one for Newbold!"

Clifton was once again in possession. The buck went left and Newbold pounced on the ball. Coming together, they wedged the ball down the field, adeptly avoiding and flattening the defending bulldozers. In a long kick, a Newbold player scored their first goal.

Clifton 4: Newbold 1

It was Newbold's ball to buck. Using hand signals of their own, they prepared for the next buck.

Gano called to his players, "Be prepared, they're going to send it deep."

The giant Kenny Ford was limping.

Kicking, Newbold took control with a set play and another flying wedge of their own. They moved the ball down the field fast. Again, a player fell injured and was dragged off the field by nearby spectators. A referee disqualified a Newbold player on the three-punch rule. Nonetheless, arriving at the goal with a wedge of their own, Newbold scored again.

Clifton 4: Newbold 2

Newbold got the mount and kicked off, as the Clifton players argued about position, Newbold moved the ball quickly down the field. With a long kick between the goals, they scored another quick goal.

Clifton 4: Newbold 3

Exhausted, both teams were bruised and worn.

Realizing the game ball had deflated, Joseph called "time out." A ball boy was summoned to inflate the pigskin ball. Carefully and quickly, the boy unlaced the four-panel leather cover, inserted a white clay pipe into the neck of the pig bladder, and with all his might, blew and blew through the pipe, inflating the ball. Looking at his dad, Stephen Jr. acknowledged the memories they shared of their first visit to Lindon's and the years he had been the ball boy who blew up the pig bladder at games. Stephen Sr. nodded his reply.

With the bladder sufficiently inflated and laces tied, the ferocious game resumed. There were ten men left on the Clifton team, and eleven on the Newbold team.

Captain Gano shouted, "Let's get that ball back men! I'm telling you right now, I'm gonna end this contest once and for all! Bust their wedge up, Big Kenny Ford!"

Bloodied and bruised, limp and all, the giant was eager to oblige.

A Newbold player kicked to his outside fielders. One picked up the ball, while the others formed another running wedge. Kenny Ford knew he needed to get to them before they gained momentum. With utmost concentration and unwavering determination the big man running hard busted through their wedge and picked up the vulnerable frightened runner and pile drived him hard to the ground, bouncing the ball out of his hands and body.

Kenny then lateralled it on one bounce, to the legendary captain who picked up the ball and ran with it. With the Newbold players closing in, Stephen Gano Sr. sprinted toward the lightly guarded goal. Just to be safe, as he got close, he lateralled the ball to an open teammate. Stephen Jr. scored easily.

Clifton 5: Newbold 3, Game over.

At that moment, thinking Stephen Sr. still had the ball, the two Newbold players hit him head on, causing all three to collapse to the ground. Shaking off the hard hit, the two Newbolders began to slowly rise. As the Clifton mates circled their legendary captain shouting triumphant congratulations, it became obvious that Stephen Sr. was not moving.

Between denial and hope, a Clifton teammate exclaimed, "Captain, you did it again! We won! You won it again!"

Combining efforts with his hero to score the winning goal, Stephen Gano Jr. was euphoric. Eager to celebrate, he ran to where his dad lay motionless, blood trickling from his ear. Stephen Jr. knew immediately something was terribly wrong. Terrified, he fought back the tears.

"Father, are you ok?" Stephen Jr. pleaded, kneeling at his side. "You are strong! You're okay Pa, you're strong!" As the tears trickled down his cheek, Stephen Jr. demanded desperately, "Get up! Get up! Get up Papa!!! Please!"

Members of both teams fetched a bucket of water and poured it on Stephen Sr. head hoping it would shock him into awareness. In an equal surge, seeing no response from his father, Stephen Jr.'s trickle of tears turned into a full out waterfall of emotion.

Someone yelled for a doctor. An older man with glasses ran from the sidelines onto the field. Identifying himself as a physician, the man proceeded to lift Stephen Sr.'s wrist, checking for a pulse. He pulled up his eyelids, scanning for a reaction from the pupils. Then put his ear to his heart.

Shaking his head left to right, the doctor shouted, "Let's get this man to the infirmary, fast! Bring a wagon!"

After what seemed an eternity, a food vendor's horse drawn wagon arrived on the field. Team members lifted Stephen Sr.'s lifeless body and laid it down on the wooden planks. Stephen Jr. and his Uncle Jack climbed in alongside, as did the doctor. As the wagon pulled away, grown men could be seen sobbing. The crowd from the game followed on horseback, wagon and foot.

News of Stephen Gano's condition spread fast. Before the wagon arrived at the small, rural, county infirmary, Gano's wife and daughters were waiting. It didn't take long before many of the townspeople were at the small hospital as well.

As the wagon carrying her husband pulled up to the small building, Jeanne Gano ran to meet it. Though she had already cried many tears, nothing could prepare her for what she saw. Her tears accelerated and her wails could no doubt be heard for miles.

Through her tears, Jeanne Gano screamed, "No, no, not now! I told you not to Rumble! Now what? Now what?" What will I do?

The crowd of townspeople watched, and cried, and prayed.

Fear and agony overcame Jeanne Gano as she moved closer to her husband's limp body. She didn't know if he was alive or dead as she repeated, "What will I do? What will I do now?"

Running to the wagon as well, Morgan and Carly held tight to their mom as Stephen Jr. stepped down to join them. Leaning in, Jeanne hugged her husband gently and sobbed. Fearing the worst and with despair consuming her, she cried, "My love! My love! What will I do? What will I do now? What will I do without you? What about our children?"

Looking up, Jeanne saw a crowd of people gathered. She kissed Stephen Sr. on the forehead, and then dropped to her knees. Surrounded, she prayed, "Please Lord, please don't take my husband. He promised me this would be his last Rumble but this is not what he meant." Please Lord, Please don't take him now.

Saying those words, Jeanne grabbed her children and hugged them tightly. Looking into their eyes she saw their terrible pain and whispered, "God, give us strength."

Praying and crying, the mass of people assembled grew larger with each passing minute. Carriages, wagons, and buggies arrived, along with men on horses and men on foot. Everyone wanted to see the legendary footballer and pray for his recovery. Surrounded by love and support, the Gano family faced the inevitable. After being brought into the small hospital it became official that the legendary Stephen George Gano Sr. had died.

CHAPTER 6

AT THE FUNERAL A LARGE CROWD GATHERED AROUND THE
Gano family. Dressed in black, with heads hung low, Jeanne, Morgan, Carly
Ann, and Stephen Jr. faced the casket. A priest stood ready for the service as
bagpipes played in the background suddenly stopped.

Speaking to the family and the crowd assembled to support them, the
priest began to pray:

*Today, we grieve the death of our beloved Stephen Gano, Sr. He was a man
who put God first, family second, and his mates a close third. To the eyes of most
people, Stephen had everything a man could ever want, and indeed, he did.*

*He had a loving wife, Jeanne and three beautiful children, Morgan, Stephen Jr,
and Carly Ann. He loved his family deeply, had the respect of an entire community,
and, as evidenced by the crowd gathered, enjoyed abundant love from friends and
acquaintances alike.*

*This legendary footballer appreciated everything and everyone and took noth-
ing for granted. He was a special man, a mate of mates, a husband, father, brother,
and friend. He died playing the game he loved. He will be sorely missed, but never
forgotten. Stephen often said, "Never let what you were in your past limit who you
can become in your future." He was a grand example of what a man can become.*

*We cannot know the reasons our beloved Stephen has been taken so soon from
this earth, but with our faith in you, our Lord, we are comforted in the knowledge
he is with you.*

*May God bless you, Stephen Gano Sr., and may you rest in eternal peace.
May God bless your family. May God bless your mates and all who loved you and
whom you loved. Amen*

The crowd repeated, "Amen."

As the crowd slowly dispersed, lumber and coal mining executives and other business owners huddled together. One man broke from the pack and approached Jeanne.

"Excuse me, Mrs. Gano," said the man, "My name is Jonathan Marshall.

Looking up, Jeanne acknowledged Jonathan with a nod.

"Pardon me for the intrusion, ma'am, and my deepest condolences to you and your family. Stephen was a great man," Jonathan offered. Pointing to the group of men standing off in the distance, he continued, "Those men and I have been talking, and we want you to know that we have agreed to honor Stephen by helping you and the children financially and in any way that is needed."

Shocked and overwhelmed, through her tears, Jeanne reacted, "Thank you, but we will survive somehow. I can't take your charity. My husband would never have allowed it."

Jonathan asserted, "Now we won't hear a word of that. This is a terrible tragedy and we will help. The arrangements have already been made, so we'll not accept another mention of this matter, ma'am."

Grateful, embarrassed and numb, Jeanne nodded again as she thanked Jonathan for the kindness he and the others had shown her. Feeling broken, as Jonathan walked away, she grabbed her daughters' hands and rushed toward the wagon that would take them home.

Stephen Jr. stood alone by his father's grave, paralyzed as he stared at the casket in which his father lay. Joseph, the Newbold captain, approached him respectfully.

"Junior," Joseph began, pulling a ball out of a burlap bag, "this is the pigskin from the game. Every man on both squads signed it. Your dad was supposed to have it. Not only was he the captain of the winning team, but the two of you scored the winning goal. In his stead, we want you to have it." Joseph handed the ball to Stephen Jr.

Looking at the pigskin, Stephen Jr. replied, "Mr. Griggs, my father would have given it to another of his mates who was more deserving than he. Maybe you should give it to someone else."

Struck by young Stephen's humility, Joseph noted, "There is no one more deserving than you, lad. Keep it as a reminder of how great a man your father was and how well you worked together on that football field. We've truly lost a great, great man."

Stephen Jr. shook his head in agreement as he accepted the game ball.

Feeling she had given him enough time, Jeanne Gano left the girls in the wagon and went to retrieve her son. Seeing the ball in his hands, she looked directly into his eyes and spoke, "Junior?"

"Yes, Mother," Stephen Jr. obediently responded.

"Promise me, Stephen Gano Jr., that you will never Rumble again, so long as I am on this good earth."

Blinking away tears, Stephen Jr. took a deep breath and replied, "I promise, Mother, you have my word I promise."

In that moment, the sacrifice Stephen Jr. made was beyond what anyone could appreciate. The game was in his blood. He desperately wanted to keep playing, not only for himself, but also to honor his father's legacy. His dad had been a great player, one of the greatest. His promise smothered a flame that burned hot in his soul. And yet, Stephen Jr. knew he couldn't deny his mother's wish.

Stephen's brother, Peter, opening a letter postmarked Rugby, England is sitting in his Boston home reading and crying from the loss of his older brother, a man he loved and admired. It didn't take long to resolve that he would step in to take care of Jeanne and the children. Stephen Jr. would be completing his last year at Rugby School and would soon be ready to begin college. Peter vowed to help his nephew attend one of the finest colleges available: Harvard, Yale, The College of New Jersey or Rutgers.

Peter telegraphed a message back to Jeanne, expressing his sorrow and condolences. He said he wanted her and the children to move to the states once Stephen Jr. completed his schooling at Rugby. He would provide everything they needed and help, as much as possible, to make the transition as easy as possible.

CHAPTER 7

IN JUNE 1858, STEPHEN JR. COMPLETED HIS LAST YEAR AT Rugby School. It had been almost a year since Stephen Gano Sr. passed away. Standing at London Harbor, waiting to board a steam ship to the United States of America, the Gano family was saying their goodbyes to family and friends. As they braced against overwhelming fear of the unknown, they also pushed back the pain of leaving all they had known and loved. The thunderous boarding horn sounded as they held onto the last precious moments with their loved ones.

In attendance, Stephen Jr.'s longtime girlfriend wiped away tears as he took her in his arms. "I'll return for you after my studies, Kathleen," he assured her.

With tears rolling down her cheeks, rubbing the promise ring Stephen Jr. had given her, she managed to choke out, "I'll be counting the days."

The last signal for boarding echoed through the air. Jeanne and her three children quietly turned and joined the crowd walking up the gangway to the steamship. Once on the boat, people gathered around the railing, waving their last goodbyes to the throngs of friends and family on the pier.

In short order, the ship began to move. Once they were no longer able to see the well-wishers on the pier, the Gano family left the rail and went in search of their modest living quarters. Peter had secured their berth, a small suite on the middle level with double bunk beds. Small, but clean and comfortable, it was home for their twenty-one-day trip across the Atlantic.

Once settled, Jeanne looked adoringly at her son and said, "I'm so proud of you, Stephen. Your father, God bless his soul, would have been proud as well. Thanks to Uncle Peter we will have a great life in Boston, and you will continue to make us proud.

"Once we settle in, you will visit the schools that have offered you enrollment. Then you'll select the one you want to attend. It's not easy to be accepted, Stephen. You worked hard and have achieved so much already."

"Mum, I'm really excited," replied Stephen Jr. "Even though you think I was distracted, I've always wanted to study in the United States, ever since I was a young lad. I just hope I can keep up."

"Of course you'll be able to keep up, Stephen!" his mother fussed. "You've always done what you put your mind to doing. This'll be no different. And if you ever doubt yourself, just remember what your father taught ya."

Nodding somberly, Stephen thought about the words he'd heard his father say so often in his young life, "A pure effort leaves no regret." Then he reassured her, "I know I'll be fine, Mum."

Picturing his father running down the field, dragging players who tried to bring him down, Stephen Jr. said to himself, "I won't let you down, Pa."

In a moment of raw emotion, Stephen Jr. grabbed his sisters and mother in a generous hug. Embracing in their small cabin, each considered what adventures the "new world" would bring.

Almost three weeks later, a loud steam horn bellowed out a cheerful hello, waking anyone still asleep on the three hundred-passenger steamship. Most passengers had been up for hours, excitedly lining the railing, watching the United States of America come into view. As the boat pulled up to Constitution Wharf in Boston Harbor, the crowd was anxious and excited to get off the boat.

Having gathered their suitcases, the Gano family awaited their turn to disembark. Searching through the crowds, the Ganos anxiously sought their American family. Shouts surrounded Jeanne and her children as new arrivals connected with family and friends. Finally hearing her name, Jeanne turned to see her brother in law, Peter, and his wife, Sarah wildly waving their arms. In tow were their three young children.

Peter and his family quickly made their way to Jeanne and the children and greeted them with kisses and big hugs. It reminded Jeanne of the family hugs she and her family enjoyed. But there was no time to think. Within moments, they were moving away from the crowd toward the horse drawn carriage waiting to take them home. Peter helped load their bags as the women and children took their seats. In short order they were on their way "uptown." The clickity clack of metal horseshoes on cobblestone was oddly soothing.

Seated in front, Peter turned to the family with a smile. "There's so much to ask," he said, "I don't know where to start. Junior, you look just like my brother, God rest his soul. Morgan and Carly Ann, thank goodness you look like your mum. Just beautiful! We're so glad you're all here." What a tragedy, my brother was a great man.

Considering what to say next, Peter continued, "So Junior, what subjects are you interested in? I hear you're a great mathematician and are curious about the engineering of things. I also enjoy learning about the history of things as well, Junior replied.

"I'm not sure what I want to study, Uncle Peter. I like so many things. So, I'm leaving the decision open," Stephen responded. "I think I'd like to see Harvard first, then Yale, and then look at the College of Colonel Rutgers. After I see all three, I'll then decide."

"That's how I reckoned it as well," Peter confirmed. "You'll have a great deal of fun visiting the colleges. I'll tell you; Harvard was a hoot when I was there." They all offer a great Victorian education. When we lived in Neshanic, New Jersey before moving to Boston we loved going to the Raritan Bay near Rutgers to fish. It's a great area and Rutgers is a great College. You know Stephen, if your parents moved to the States when I did, you would have been born there.

"Harvard keeps you close to family, Stephen," Jeanne encouraged, already missing the familiarity of home and not wanting Stephen far.

"I know, Mum, but I really want to see all the schools and decide which one is best for me," Stephen asserted.

As the family pulled up to the gated stone house belonging to Peter Gano, they were awestruck. Built in Boston's Beacon Hill, a community of affluence, the home was not just beautiful, but also substantial in size.

As everyone got out of the carriage, Peter offered, "The house should serve you quite well, Jeanne. You'll find there's plenty of room for all of us, and it's well-appointed for guests."

Stephen could hardly contain himself, "Wow, Uncle Peter, this is the most beautiful house I've ever seen! There must be a lot of gold in trading coal!"

"My boy," boasted Uncle Peter, "one day coal will run the world! My partners and I have done a good job of selling that idea, and we've been handsomely rewarded. That ship you were on; it used coal for fuel."

"Don't let him fool you, Stephen," warned his mother. "Your Uncle Peter failed plenty before he found success. Just like your father always told you, 'a pure effort leaves no regret.' Uncle Peter persevered, despite his setbacks."

Sarah added, "Stephen, he had us living on a few dollars a month. Why, some of his crazy ideas nearly sent us to the poorhouse. We found that with faith in God and hard work, anything is possible. In fact, everything is possible!" But at times his stubbornness bordered on stupidness.

Uncle Peter chimed in, "Remember Junior, the difference between insanity and genius is success! This isn't called 'land of the free, home of the brave' for nothing. In this country, we are free from government restrictions that prevent us from pursuing our dreams. If you're brave enough to follow your instinct and take a chance, you can create your own grand destiny. These United States were built on a foundation of freedom and liberty. People who want to take risks and make money and people who want to fish all day are equally entitled. And then there are the few who will figure out how to make money by fishing all day. Now that's what I call freedom!"

Uncle Peter was silent for a moment, then resumed, "It takes discipline and determination to reach your dreams. This country fought for its independence from a tyrannical government. They said 'no' to the crooked English government that promised liberty, only to increase taxes and decrease freedom. You are better off counting on yourself than counting on the government. They call it free market capitalism. Individuals have the freedom to capitalize on their ideas and create opportunities for themselves. On the other hand, capitalism can be a cruel disciplinarian if your idea fails, so be careful when venturing out."

Seemingly on a roll, Peter continued, "Another important trait is perseverance. You have to keep trying, even if you fail you learn. As Sarah told you, I failed plenty, but I always got back to business."

CHAPTER 8

SEVERAL MONTHS PASSED. STEPHEN AND HIS FAMILY WERE adjusting quite well to life in Boston. The new semester would soon be starting, and Stephen was beginning to consider which college he would attend.

One evening at dinner, Uncle Peter handed Stephen an envelope and announced, "Here's your train schedule, and money for your travels, Junior. I've made all the arrangements. The colleges are expecting you. Once you've made your decision, we will arrange for you to get your belongings, and I'll send additional money." The College of New Jersey has not responded to my request. So Harvard, Yale and Rutgers will be the colleges you choose from.

With the etiquette of a socialite, Stephen said, "Thank you Uncle Peter, for all the wisdom, love, and support. You have been a great help to my mother, my sisters, and myself. And now you are helping me to get an education that will allow me to help my family as well. I promise to make you proud, and I will not forget your generosity. "

With that, Peter gave Stephen a big bear hug. Jeanne and the girls joined him.

Stephen Jr. dressed in his Sunday finest, donning a crisp suit, small suitcase and proper hat. Arriving early, he stood in Harvard Yard taking in the sights and sounds. It was October, and the autumn leaves were turning magnificent shades of red, yellow, and orange as they tried in vain to cling to their branches. Students were already on campus, preparing for the semester's November start. There were boys of all shapes and sizes reading, eating, strolling, or scurrying to this building or that.

As he walked, Stephen spotted a football game in play. Watching for a moment, he recalled playing with his dad and sighed. Moving closer, he spotted a boy sitting on a bordering fence, watching the game.

Approaching the well-dressed young man, Stephen asked, "Excuse me, do you know where Harvard Hall is located? I'm scheduled to meet with a professor there."

"Why you're right upon it," the young man responded, pointing to the building behind them. "The Beantown wind must have knocked the sign down."

Coyly, Stephen pointed at the game in play and asked, "They play football here?"

The young man responded, "Boston Rules Football."

"Looks a lot like the game my father and I used to play," Stephen commented, "except there are so few men on the teams. What are the numbers?"

As they talked, Stephen watched one of the squads effortlessly move the ball down the field. By the looks of their laterals and running plays, they were a well-oiled machine.

The young man answered, "Twelve on a squad. The Oneida club hasn't lost a game in four years. They're Beantown's best footballers. See the 'O's' stitched on their jerseys?"

"Wow," Stephen admired, "they sure seem to have good strategies!"

Hearing Stephen's accent. "You're not from around here are you?" the young man inquired.

Stephen shook his head "no."

Graciously, the young man offered more information to the eager newcomer, explaining, "Oneida was a local Indian tribe. They were said to shape shift to evade the enemy."

Pointing to a boy mid field, the man continued, "Gerritt Miller, that tall, lanky guy... he captains the team. People call him 'Gat.' He's fearless."

The two watched the action for a moment. Then the boy offered, "Did you know we call Boston 'Beantown'? And do you know why?"

Not waiting for an answer, the man went on, "It's because of our overwhelming affinity for our black beans cooked in molasses. The early sailors that passed through our ports loved the dish and demanded it upon every stop. They coined the term "Beantown" and it stuck.

So where are you from?" Stephen listened intently, never taking his eyes off the game being played. Politely, he responded, "I'm from a small village called Clifton Upon Dunsmore in Rugby, England."

As he watched the game, Stephen realized it was an intriguing variation on the rougher version of Rugby he'd played back home. Observing the captain giving a variety of hand signals, Stephen added, "Man, that 'Gat' really gets it! He has some good plays."

"Yes," agreed the young man, "He designs 'em better than anyone."

Nodding, Stephen realized he was going to be late to his meeting. He thanked the young man, turned, and headed toward Harvard Hall. It was hard for him to keep his eyes away from the game.

"I'll see you around, then," Stephen remarked to the young man as he took his leave.

Hurrying to his meeting, Stephen noted a professor coming his way. With a tall stovepipe hat, the elder was unmistakable. As proper etiquette dictated, passing five rods (eighty feet) from a professor, Stephen tipped his hat.

Continuing on his way, still half watching the game behind him, Stephen tripped over a large burlap bag as he approached the steps to Harvard Hall. Distracted, he thought he saw movement in the bag, but quickly convinced himself he was just nervous about his meeting. He walked up the steps and used the heavy, brass door knocker to bang on the large wooden door. Confused, he glanced back at the moving burlap.

The door opened. Once again, tipping his hat to an elder, Stephen greeted, "Good day! I'm looking for Professor Thomas Hill, please. I'm Stephen Gano from England."

The professor nodded and smiled at Stephen. Acknowledging that he was the professor in question, he shook Stephen's hand firmly and invited him into the building. Unable to stop thinking about what he saw, or didn't see, Stephen kept looking back to the burlap bag. He apologized for his confusion.

Peering around Stephen to the bag, the professor chuckled. "Oh those freshmen," he began, "they never learn why the upperclassmen want to enter them in the sack race with their hands tied, their eyes blindfolded, and a sock stuck in their mouths. They always figure it out a bit too late."

With that, the professor walked over to the jiggling bag, opened it, and removed the blindfold and sock from the young man's mouth inside the sack. Retrieving a knife from his pocket, he cut the boy's hand and leg ties. Drenched in sweat and gasping for air, the boy nodded graciously and then ran without uttering a word.

"It's an annual freshman hazing gag," explained the professor. "They always do this shortly before the semester begins, but they usually knock on the door before leaving the sac. Well maybe they did knock, could be I didn't hear it. Glad we got him out when we did. That boy was definitely in the bag much too long."

A bit shocked by what he had just witnessed, Stephen tried to compose himself.

"I've been looking forward to meeting you," Professor Hill began. "Your Uncle has told me great things about you. You should be very proud of your accomplishments. Come, sit," he said, gesturing toward a large, leather chair with his hand.

Unable to clear his thoughts from the game he was watching, Stephen asked, "Do you allow football to be played here at Harvard?"

No, not anymore. "Too many serious injuries," the professor answered, shaking his head. "That devilish pastime was banned almost forty years ago. They used to split the student body by last name. First half of the alphabet on one team, second on the other. The games were too violent. Believe it or not, we had a football burial ceremony on campus with a song and all to make the ban official."

'Beneath this sod we lay you down. This sign of glorious fight. With dismal groans and yells we'll drown. Your mournful burial rite.'

"I understand why," Stephen said in agreement.

Having noticed Stephen's interest in the game outside, Professor Thomas continued, "The Oneida Club uses Harvard Yard when Boston Commons is too crowded. They'll take on anyone willing to challenge them and they'll play anywhere there's space. The Harvard students are only allowed to watch."

Noting Stephen's significant distractedness, the professor got up and went to the window, inviting Stephen to do the same. As they watched the game from afar, Stephen saw a play he hadn't seen before: Two men interlocked their arms then flung a third smaller and lighter fellow forward. What is that play? Stephen asked. A" fling wedge" the professor answered back, an Oneida club original play, it works most of the time.

Shaking his head, the professor remarked, "They always play a vicious running game. There aren't many students who could survive the brutality."

Eager to engage Stephen in the sights and sounds of Harvard, the professor offered, "We do allow what we call 'Bloody Monday.' The first Monday of every fall semester, the upperclassmen like nothing better than to plant the cocky freshmen in the Harvard Yard sod. It's a football game of sorts, a vicious game. The upperclassmen have one main strategy. They are more concerned with assaulting the freshmen's shins than kicking the football."

"Sounds brutal," Stephen remarked.

"It can be," agreed the professor. "Now, would you like to see the campus?"

"I'd like that very much, Professor Hill," Stephen replied.

Walking out of Harvard Hall, both men had their eyes fixed on the Oneida team and the game being played. The professor allowed Stephen to watch for a few minutes and then ushered him down a path away from the game.

As they toured the oldest college campus in the United States, the professor began, "Did you know this college was founded in 1636 by John Harvard?" He also left upon his death his volume of 400 books that started the Harvard Library, the oldest library in the United States.

Starting with some interesting history, Professor Hill took Stephen to see the country's first printing press, dating back to 1638. As they walked, he explained that there were currently 280 students in attendance at Harvard, and that each year that number grew. He pointed to the various buildings that comprised the school, asking questions to gauge Stephens's interests.

"Do you know our college motto?" the professor asked.

Stephen shook his head "no," so the professor continued, "It's 'VERITAS' which means 'truth'."

"Chronos, the daughter of Saturn, said living a truthful life is what makes a fulfilling life," Stephen remarked. "I like that a lot." That's a great way to interpret it, the Professor responds.

The two walked past Massachusetts Hall, then Memorial Hall, which was erected to honor the Union soldiers. Venturing beyond the school, Professor Hill showed Stephen the Bell in Hand Tavern, as well as the surrounding neighborhood. The area was burgeoning, as evidenced by the construction sites visible wherever they looked.

Returning to Harvard Hall, Professor Hill encouraged, "Stephen Gano, we would love to have you join our ranks. I think you would fit in quite well."

Thanking the professor, Stephen responded, "I have two more colleges to visit, sir. I'll let you know of my decision by next week."

With a handshake, the two parted ways.

Leaving Harvard, Stephen went directly to the train station. He boarded a train to New Haven, Connecticut. Arriving late in the evening, he lodged overnight at a local tavern. He visited Yale the following day. Similar to his experience at Harvard, one of the professors showed him the beautiful campus while describing its rich history as they toured the campus and the surrounding area, explaining how "Mob Football" was once played on the New Haven town green pitting the freshman against the sophomores until it was banned in 1858 for its violence and numerous injuries. With his Yale tour completed, early that evening, he was at the train station once again.

Standing near the rails, with his suitcase in hand, Stephen awaited the next train to New York City. It was getting cold outside. He had been wait ing for what seemed like hours. Finally, the crowded, five-car train arrived. Stephen boarded, stowed his suitcase, settled in and went to sleep. It had been a long couple of days.

CHAPTER 9

"NEXT STOP NEW YORK CITY; NEW YORK CITY, NEXT STOP," boomed the conductor. "NEW YORK CITY, NEXT STOP!"

Startling awake, Stephen quickly gathered his wits and grabbed his belongings. When the train came to a complete stop, the doors opened, and he exited. He looked around, seeking someone who might assist him in navigating the train schedule for the next leg of his trip.

Stephen spotted a conductor standing near the tracks. He rushed up to the man and blurted, "Excuse me sir, can you help me figure out when the next train to New Bruns..."

'Can't you see I'm speaking with the conductor?' an irritated young woman reprimanded.

Flustered, Stephen replied. "Excuse me, miss. I apologize. I didn't notice you."

Stephen blushed now seeing this beautiful, voluptuous brunette. How could he not notice her, he thought.

Seemingly irritated with the conductor, the woman resumed her interrogation, asking, "Why aren't you more helpful with this schedule? Who can understand all these times and places?"

"Miss, I have no control over the promptness of the rails. I apologize for the cow," the conductor said. Directing her to the train coming into the station, he added, "You'll want to take that night owl to Philadelphia. It stops at Princeton.

Stephen waited patiently for the woman to move on, and then inquired, "Can you direct me to a train that will take me to New Brunswick, New Jersey?"

"That would be the same train our feisty southern belle is taking," the conductor said pointing after her. He advised, "It stops in New Brunswick before Princeton. Expect a two to three hour ride."

"Thank you, sir," Stephen said, as he rushed to get on the train.

On the train, curious about the 'southern belle' he was told to follow, Stephen stowed his suitcase near hers. He sat across from her, gathering his confidence to speak. The woman, definitively disinterested, picked up a book, shifted a bit to get comfortable, and began to read.

Time passed and finally the woman looked up from her book long enough for Stephen to notice her aqua blue eyes. Seeking to strike up a conversation, "I-I'm sorry for the interruption... with the conductor, miss."

As if sparking a fire, the woman erupted, "Well you should be. I had been waiting two hours for this train to finally arrive! A delay on the tracks they told me... a pregnant cow on the tracks! Can you believe that? Two hours of a stubborn cow laying on the blooming tracks!"

Stephen wondered if he'd made a mistake engaging the apparent "church-bell" before him.

The woman shook her head and a subtle smile crossed her face. She continued, "If it was a bull, they would have just shot it right then and there and dragged its dead carcass off the tracks in a flash. But no, a bloomin' pregnant cow who refused to get off the tracks, and I had to wait!"

"I Sure am glad I'm not a bull," Stephen teased, holding back a smile.

Recognizing the kindness in Stephen's manner and the playfulness in his remark, the woman smiled coyly and reconsidered, "Well, maybe a little more prodding was in order. Two hours is a long time to wait!"

"Where are you from," the woman asked, noticing Stephen's accent.

"A village in Rugby, England, miss. I'm Stephen Gano Jr.," he said, offering his hand. "Glad to meet your acquaintance, miss."

"Marianne Glen," she said, putting her hand in his for a gentle shake. "Pleasure to meet you as well."

"So what were you doing in New York City, Miss Glen?" Stephen probed.

"Well," Marianne began, "I went to visit my aunt and uncle. But I wouldn't be in the northeast at all if I had a choice. I'm from the south. North Carolina to be specific, can you tell?"

Reconsidering her question, Marianne said, "Well, maybe not since you're not from these parts. Anyway, my mama, brother, and I moved to Princeton after the war. Our farm was destroyed the same day my daddy was killed trying to protect us from Yankee soldiers. We couldn't rebuild by ourselves, so we moved north. My mama has a brother in Princeton. He has a beautiful little farm there, and so now we live with him. So now we have to live amongst them darned Yankees."

"I'm sorry to hear about your losses," Stephen offered. "How is your family getting along?"

"It was really bad for a while," Marianne remembered. "I loved my daddy so much. Things will never be the same without him, but we've made peace with it. He'll always be with us." She put her hand on her heart and looked skyward.

"Yes, I know he will be," Stephen said in agreement. "So how did you come to be at the train station all alone?" he questioned.

"Well, like I said before, I was visiting my aunt and uncle, another of mama's brothers," Marianne explained. "They brought me to the train station for my return to Princeton, but when the train was delayed indefinitely, I told them to leave me. I didn't see any reason for us all to wait for a pregnant cow!"

Enjoying the conversation, Marianne and Stephen smiled, and then Marianne asked, "What about you? What are you doing on this train?"

"I'm visiting colleges," Stephen responded. "I went to Harvard first, then Yale, and now I'm headed to New Brunswick, New Jersey to visit Rutgers College. I have to decide where I want to study."

"Oh," Marianne reacted, "your mother must be so proud of you! Not everyone gets admitted to the colonial colleges! And you have your choice!"

Bowing his head with humility, Stephen acknowledged, "She is."

"My brother William nicknamed "Tar Heel" was a soldier for the south during the war. Now he's one of the "men of Nassau", a student at the College of New Jersey in Princeton. How's that for a twist of fate?" Marianne jokes.

"Whew, that's quite a twist," Stephen said.

Marianne asked, "Are you visiting there, too?

"I submitted my transcripts," Stephen answered. "They haven't responded. I heard Princeton is one of the nicest villages in the whole northeast. My uncle said they have some of the best architecture and farmland in the country. Is your brother enjoying his studies at the College of New Jersey?"

"Yes, I think he likes it fine," Marianne remarked. "But he tells me his professors are looking for perfection in his Greek to Latin translations. He's not so good at that. The whole college thing is a lot of work. The semester starts in November and ends in April, with a few breaks for the holidays. Then there is an optional summer semester that runs from May to September. His school days start at 6:00 a.m. and end at 10:00 p.m. They get breaks for meals and some recreation, but it's a demanding schedule full of reading, studying and tutors. His favorite part of school seems to be playing on the Princeton Nine baseball team. The team is famous, you know! When they are short a fellow, sometimes I practice with them."

"What's baseball?" asked Stephen.

"Oh, I'm sorry, I thought you'd know!" Marianne commented, surprised by Stephen's ignorance on the subject. "There are two teams that play against each other. Each team has nine players. A pitcher tries to throw a horsehair filled, cowhide covered ball past a batter who tries to hit it with a wooden bat. Most of the time they miss, but when they hit, the players in the field try to catch the ball with leather mittens. If they do, it's an out. If the batter misses with a swing three times, it's also an out. Each team gets three outs before they switch from batting to fielding and vice versa. When they hit the ball, they have to run around four bases. That's how they score. There's more to it, but you get the idea. Once you play a few times, you'll understand completely."

Marianne paused for a moment and then continued, "It's kind of exciting, actually. And sometimes I can hit the ball further than some of the boys!"

"Wow! They let you fill in?" Stephen asked, marveling at the idea. "I'll have to look into it." Moving on, Stephen asked, "How have you adjusted to life in the north? Do you like being a Yankee?"

"First of all, I'm no Yankee! And no, I don't love it here. For one, the weather is a lot colder," Marianne responded. "It snows here! I never saw snow back in North Carolina. Didn't know what it was. Sometimes it snows a whole lot. And I have a lot of chores here! Back in North Carolina we had servants for those. I have to take care of the crops! I have to admit, though, I kinda like it, especially the pumpkins in the fall."

"My dad always told me 'hard work always pays off' but you just don't know when," Marianne said.

"Wow, my father used to say the same thing!" Stephen exclaimed.

"NEW BRUNSWICK STATION; PRINCETON, NEXT STOP," shouted the conductor.

Startled, Stephen quickly stood. "This is my station," he uttered. "I'm sure glad to have met you Miss Marianne Glen. Thanks for riding the night owl with me."

"I hope you make the right decision about where to study Mr. Stephen Gano Jr.," Marianne responded. "Best of luck to ya."

Stephen extended his hand and Marianne offered hers in return. Their eyes met as they gently shook. "Thank you, Miss Glen. I wish you and your family all the best," Stephen said.

Tripping, he retrieved his suitcase and moved awkwardly toward the door. Before stepping off, he looked back at the beautiful woman he'd just met. She was looking at him as well and offered a shy smile.

As Stephen lingered in their moment of quiet connection, a group of boisterous young boys boarded the train and aggressively pushed him aside. Half rats, the boys surrounded Marianne. Menacingly, they twirled their rattan canes, pushing the copper handles toward Stephen. Had it been four years earlier, they likely would have wielded swords, but fortunately things had changed since the Civil War.

Looking at Stephen up and down one fellow shouted, "Is that foreigner bothering you Miss Marianne?"

Considering the way the men were dressed in black jackets and stove-pipe hats, Stephen understood how easily they identified him as a foreigner. He wore a proper brown jacket and top hat.

"Not at all," Marianne answered. "Stephen, these are some of my brother's teammates."

No one offered his hand to shake. Protectively, they glared at Stephen, giving him the evil eye. They moved toward him, trying to intimidate him.

Needing to exit the train, Stephen said to Marianne, "I'm glad to see you're well protected. I hope to see you in Princeton someday."

Condescendingly, one of the men said, "You just stay here with the Queensmen. Looks like you'll fit right in."

Stephen got off the train wondering what the man meant. As he walked away, he heard the conductor shout, "PRINCETON JUNCTION NEXT; LAST STOP PHILADELPHIA."

CHAPTER 10

GETTING OFF THE TRAIN IN PRINCETON, MARIANNE SEARCHED for the carriage containing her mother, Ida, and her brother, "Tar Heel". Spotting Marianne first, "Tar Heel" rushed to greet her. He grabbed her bag and helped her up into the carriage. Once they were both seated, the carriage began to move.

Marianne's family was eager to hear all about her trip to the big city. Excitedly, her mother questioned, "How was your trip? And your unescorted train ride?"

"Well, you made it back alive, so I guess it wasn't all bad," "Tar Heel" teased. "So, how was it?"

Seeming to have forgotten all about the unfortunate incident with the cow, Marianne replied, "It was most wonderful! Everyone was so pleasant and accommodating. Aunt Lilly and Uncle Wayne are quite generous. Your brother is very much like you, Mother. I also met a well mannered Englishman on the train ride home."

"I'm so glad you enjoyed your time with Aunt Lilly and Uncle Wayne in New York. It's been years since I've enjoyed my big brother's company," remarked Ida, nostalgically. Registering the last comment, she turned back to Marianne and asked, "A well mannered Englishman?"

"Yes, Mama! He was quite the gentleman. He was visiting Rutgers College to see if he wanted to attend. I told him about "Tar Heel" and Princeton and the Princeton Nine.

"I'm not happy about you talking to strange boys, Marianne," Ida admonished.

"Mama, he was harmless, really. He was from England, and so well mannered and charming," Marianne defended, then insisted, "Please don't fret about me."

"You're my little girl, Marianne. Of course I'm gonna fret. I'm not ready for you to grow up, and you're so independent," Mama confessed.

"Now Mama, I'm nineteen years old. I want to explore the world and learn as much as I can. It felt good to rely on myself!" Marianne announced.

"Tar Heel" interjected, "Yes, you're so independent that my classmates think you're stuck on yourself. They call you the 'ice queen'."

"Ice queen?" Marianne asked, bemused, "What does that mean ?

"You always ignore them if they approach you. They say you're pretty on the outside, but ice cold on the inside," "Tar Heel" explained.

"Oh "Tar Heel"," responded Marianne, "your friends bore me. Their uninvited bloviating...well I could care less."

Ida interjected, "Sounds like your college buddies are smitten with your sister, "Tar Heel"."

"A smitten, I don't know why they would be," "Tar Heel" responded. "She hardly pays them any mind, unless she's filling in for one of the Nine. Then she has no problem shouting at them."

"Why should I pay those bores any mind, "Tar Heel"? I'm not interested in their attention," Marianne confirmed.

As if he hadn't heard her, "Tar Heel" continued, "They try to break through that ice, but she doesn't give them the time of day. They probably just think she's a stuck up southern belle."

Fluffing her hair and considering what her brother was saying, Marianne responded, "I really don't want their attention, but I'll try to be more polite and indulge them in some of their mindless drivel." Sarcastically she added, "Now that I'm in the north, I really don't want to seem like an ill mannered southern belle."

CHAPTER 11

AFTER DETRAINING, STEPHEN JR. WALKED THROUGH THE town of New Brunswick, taking in the modest homes, shops, and churches. A relatively small town of 11,000, it had become a trading hub, as well as home to the four buildings that comprised Rutgers College.

The Raritan River runs through New Jersey and shapes the eastern boundary of New Brunswick. Fed by the rivers, the D&R Canal connects the Delaware River in Bordentown to the Raritan River in New Brunswick, Pennsylvania coal is transported to New York City for fuel also wheat, beef, and produce travels to the ports in Philadelphia and New York. From there, goods could then make their way across the Atlantic or to any place in America.

Exhausted, Stephen wondered what he would learn about the eighty-man school he was going to explore, and whether it would persuade him to attend Rutgers College over Harvard or Yale. Looking around, he noticed a man walking along the road.

Peering through the quiet night air, Stephen gently approached the man trying not to startle him. "Excuse me sir," he said, "could you help me find Northrop's Motel and Tavern? I'm told it's on Church Street."

The man chuckled slightly, explaining that Stephen was "nearly upon it." He offered Stephen simple directions to his destination.

"Thank you kindly, sir," Stephen replied as he turned to walk in the direction the man pointed.

Within moments, Stephen found himself at the door to Northrop's. He unceremoniously checked in and found his way to his assigned room. He fell into the modest bed, exhausted.

Waking early, Stephen donned the attire of an upper class English gent: a button down, white shirt, black wool pants, boots, brown overcoat, suspenders, and a top hat. He asked the proprietor for directions and promptly left the motel. He had an appointment with a "Professor Thacket" at Olde Queens Hall. On his way, he passed horse drawn wagons transporting fruits and vegetables.

Standing in front of a majestic stone building, Stephen read the sign, "Olde Queens Hall." After knocking, he was greeted by a tall, slender man. Stephen tipped his hat politely and inquired about the professor's whereabouts.

Generously, the man said, "Ah, good morning! I am the professor you seek. You must be that lad from Scotland. Mr. Gano I presume?"

The two shook hands as Stephen explained, "Scottish blood indeed, but I'm from Rugby, England, sir."

"I stand corrected Mr. Gano. So, how was your trip to New Brunswick? And how do you like the northeastern United States so far?" The professor asked jovially.

"The northeast is beautiful. And I'm happy to be here, sir. From what I could see in the dark last night and during my walk here this morning, New Brunswick is a great town."

"Let me take you on a tour of our humble campus, lad. I think you'll find it to be great as well," invited Professor Thacket.

Thacket and Stephen walked to the well-appointed center stairwell. Professor Thacket explained, "This is Olde Queens Hall, the first building erected on this beautiful campus. Most of our classes are taught right here in this building."

Walking up the stairs, the Professor continued, "We have four floors of Olde Queens, and a 'belled copula.' The same bell that announces the start of classes, early in the morning it is also used for celebration and for incidents of mourning. We hope that the latter are rare at most."

Wide-eyed, gazing at his surroundings, Stephen said, "It's a lovely hall indeed! King George III spared no expense honoring his Queen Charlotte."

"Well, you've done your research, lad!" Thacket joyfully acknowledged. "Would history be your primary interest?"

Feeling good about the connection he seemed to enjoy with the professor, Stephen answered, "I do enjoy history quite a bit. I was thinking, however, that engineering might be my pursuit. And of course I am here to continue my seminary studies."

Hearing Stephen's interests was music to the professor's ears. He commented, "You'll enjoy our Professor Chapman a great deal. He's chairman of engineering studies. Graduating from the nearby College of New Jersey in Princeton, he's quite accomplished in the engineering sciences. He's also a wonderful local historian."

"I'm excited to meet him, sir! I'll look forward to learning as much as I can from him," Stephen responded.

The men went down the stairs and out the door of the grand hall. Walking along a short path, Professor Thacket pointed out Hertzog Hall. He explained that while most of the students lived locally in boarding rooms; about fifteen men lived on the second floor of Hertzog Hall, the Theological Seminary. Should Stephen decide to attend Rutgers, the professor told him he would live there as well. Professor Thacket also mentioned that plans for the school's first dormitory, Winant's Hall, were in the works.

Next, the professor guided Stephen past Van Nest Hall, another building where classes were held, and then to the Daniel S. Schanck Observatory, the fourth and final building that comprised Rutgers College. Standing in front of the observatory, he explained that the small, two-story, octagonal building had been built just three years prior. It contained telescopes and clocks, as well as other donated scientific equipment, and served as the school's science building.

Completing the tour, Professor Thacket turned to Stephen and asked, "Do you have any questions, Mr. Gano?"

"Yes," Stephen answered, "I do have one, sir. At the tavern where I stayed last night, I read that the Dutch hired Henry Hudson to explore the Raritan River in the 1600s. It was because of him that New Brunswick became the hub for commerce it is today. That was really interesting. I also read that Rutgers College used to be Queens College, but wondered why?"

Professor Thacket took a deep breath and asked, "Do you have time for the full history lesson?"

"Of course," Stephen said, eager to learn.

"As you read," began the professor, "In 1766 Queens College was granted a charter by the Royal Governor of New Jersey, William Franklin. Did you know he was the illegitimate son of Ben Franklin? Anyway, William Franklin was the third royal governor to be petitioned by the Dutch Reformed Church. The Dutch wanted to create their own seminary and college. The Charter resulted in Queen's College. Hence the Queeensmen.

"At the beginning of this century, the school became financially insolvent and ultimately had to close its doors. After a failed merger with The College of New Jersey, Colonel Rutgers, who was on the board of trustees of both Queens College and the College of New Jersey at one time was a generous landowner whose family was in the brewery business, had already donated land for a large Presbyterian church in New York, gave the college a $5000 grant to reopen the school. Remember the bell in the copula at Olde Queens Hall? The colonel dedicated that to our school as well at the cost of $200.

I'm sure you've guessed by now, the college was renamed in 1825 to honor Colonel Rutgers. He died five years later, leaving no additional money to the school.

Just a few years ago, in 1864, we won land-grant status under the Morrill Act. It was a vicious battle between us and our academic neighbors to the south. The College of New Jersey may not ever forgive us for it. Nonetheless, Rutgers College now has the opportunity to dramatically expand. Who knows, one day there may be a hundred buildings and thousands of students walking this campus, living and learning about the world and what lies beyond."

Listening intently and envisioning the idea of thousands of students, Stephen contributed, "With the river so close, and New York and Philadelphia just a train ride away, I can certainly imagine that happening!"

"It just takes a nod to start the ball rolling, Mr. Gano," Thacket agreed.

"I have another question," Stephen asserted. "I was wondering how often Princeton men mingle with Rutgers men?"

Professor Thacket replied, "'Mingle' would not be the correct term. There is great rivalry between the schools. The men only interact in contests to prove supremacy. Sometimes it gets vicious."

"I may have been the recipient of one of those "contests" when I got off the train in New Brunswick. A group of students from the College of New Jersey were less than thoughtful. Gee, I wonder if they were in New Brunswick looking for trouble?"

"Indeed they might have been, Mr. Gano. It happens regularly," confirmed the professor.

"That might be just the kind of excitement I would enjoy, Professor Thacket," Stephen said.

Thacket responded, "Your visit today is the first step toward success, Mr. Gano. Remember, 'gaining knowledge before experience makes for a better experience.' What do you think of our little college?"

Excitedly, Stephen replied, "I like everything I see and hear! It's a difficult choice, however."

Wanting to assist Stephen in his decision, the professor asked, "What schools are you choosing from?"

"Rutgers, Harvard, and Yale," Steven reported.

"Well, those are three fine schools! Indeed a difficult decision to make. I will emphasize that Harvard and Yale have more than twice the enrollment that we have. If you think you would enjoy a smaller, more intimate college, I can tell you Rutgers would be proud to add you to our rolls."

Feeling confident, Stephen nodded and asked, "If I want to enroll at Rutgers, what do I do next, sir?"

"I believe you just took the next step! Welcome aboard young man! I'm delighted by your decision! You're welcome to remain here. I'll arrange for you to take a room in Hertzog Hall immediately. I'll contact your uncle and tell him the good news. He'll send your necessities."

"I'm happy to be a Queensman, sir! Thank you for the tour and information, and thanks to my uncle for his help and support!" Stephen reflected.

"While I send a telegram and make arrangements for your things, I suggest you go over to Hertzog and get acquainted with your classmates."

"Thank you Professor. I'm eager to be a part of this great learning institution. I'm especially looking forward to learning in the new observatory!" Stephen said.

After shaking hands with the Professor, Stephen left Olde Queens Hall. Walking toward Hertzog to meet his cohorts, he hears a great racket of noise. Pushing the grand wooden door open, he entered the building and followed the commotion to the second floor dormitory. A group of men appeared as he reached the top of the stairs.

"Good afternoon, mates, I'm Stephen Gano Jr. from Rugby, England. I've come to join your ranks at this great college," Stephen greeted.

The first to respond was Claudius Rockefeller who was picking up a pair of dice that had strayed. Warmly, each man welcomed Stephen into the fold, offering their hand to shake. After Claudius came William Leggett, then Preston Huyssoon, George Walker, George Dixon, Winfield Lasher, Jacob Van Fleet, Daniel Mallet, and John Alfred Van Nest (whose father donated the money to build Van Nest Hall).

"Great to add another Queensman to our ranks," Winfield greeted.

Introductions complete, Preston invited the men to sit in his room. They engaged Stephen in a get-to-know and offered some detail on what Stephen might expect as a student at Rutgers.

"When we aren't studying, we try to have some fun. There's lots to do on and off campus," Jacob informed. "Sometimes we take the train to New York City, or go to a social on the shores of New Jersey. When we're looking for something a bit closer, we take the train to Princeton and see what trouble we can stir up with our college foes. Have you heard about the rivalry between the College of New Jersey and our dear Rutgers College?"

"Professor Thacket mentioned it, yes." Stephen answered. "I want to know more!"

"You will, you will," Claudius assured while tossing the dice in the air. "It's always a part of life here at Rutgers,"

"I ran into a bunch of men when I was getting off the train in New Brunswick," Stephen shared. "They weren't nice at all, real troublemaker types. I was saying goodbye to the beautiful young woman from the South

I met on the trip. They surrounded her and acted quite threatening towards me. They were definitely College of New Jersey men."

"Yeah, that sounds typical. We go there to stir up trouble, and they come here and do the same. They're mad because they think they deserved the land grant the governor gave us a few years ago," added Winfield.

William asked, "Did Thacket tell you any of the campus rules?"

"No, we didn't talk about that," Stephen answered. William responded, we are governed by the "Student Code of 1760"

"There's no dice," William said, smiling in Claudius' direction. "No card playing, no drinking, and no horses or dogs allowed anywhere on campus or in the buildings. Being caught with any of those results in financial penalties and possible expulsion. Plus there's no guns, swords, or gambling of any kind."

Looking at Claudius with a wink, William continued, "Any time you leave the campus, you have to have approval from a professor. That includes going to the river to fish. And of course, we aren't allowed to have women in the rooms."

Still thinking about Stephen's initial comments, Claudius wondered, "So, this lady on the train, tell us more. Will you see her again?"

Stephen described Marianne to the men and added, "I have a girlfriend back home in England. I gave her a promise ring and hope to marry her after I complete my studies. Her name is Kathleen."

Laughter filled the room as the men teased Stephen about his serious manner and his steadfast allegiance to Kathleen.

Your lady back home won't know a thing about your love interests here in the United States," William goaded.

"I made a promise to her," Stephen defended. "We've spoken of marriage."

Jacob, poking Stephen, firmly stated, "Well none of us has a girl. We'll have to go find this southern belle on our next Princeton excursion. Maybe she'll indulge us, too."

"Come on Stephen, I'll show you the room you'll share with Claudius," William offered. "You must be eager to settle in?"

Nodding, Stephen followed William to his room down the hall. A single dresser, a trunk, and two beds filled the small space.

Once inside, Stephen closed the door. He took a moment to consider what the day had presented. He had been in New Brunswick for barely twenty-four hours, but in that time he made the decision to attend Rutgers, making New Jersey his home for a time. It was a huge decision that would change his life forever. He wished he could share it with his dad. Opening his suitcase, he pulled out the game ball from a burlap bag that Joseph Griggs had given him from the game that took his father's life. It was as close as he could come. Comforted, he put the ball back in the bag and retrieved his bible. He began to read.

Days have past and Stephen settles in.

CHAPTER 12

"GANO, WAKE UP," WILLIAM SHOUTED AS HE BANGED ON
Stephen's door. "Morning Prayer starts in ten minutes."

It was November and the semester had begun. Startling awake, Stephen
jumped up to get ready, with Claudius already gone. He poured water from
the pitcher into the bowl that sat atop his dresser. He washed his face, quickly
got dressed, grabbed his supplies, and was out the door within the allotted
time.

Following Morning Prayer, Stephen and William walked into Olde
Queens, climbed two flights of stairs, and found their seats in the classroom.
The history lecture was just starting. Class required they pay close attention
for hours. The men were thrilled when the professor announced that it was
time for lunch.

Outside in the brisk air, Stephen and his classmates released their
pent-up energy. Running races and a kicking contest ruled the moment, and
Stephen was thrilled to be a part of them.

Leggett and Rockefeller watched as Stephen outran and outkicked
most of the others. Impressed, Leggett called, "Gano, you're quite the athlete!
How'd you keep it hidden these last couple of weeks?"

Humbly, Stephen answered, "We played a lot of games back home. I
got my skills from my father. He was a legendary footballer."

Joining William and Claudius, Stephen sat down. They wanted to
know all about Stephen's father, but Stephen wouldn't speak a word about
him. With little time left before starting the next round of classes, Claudius
changed the subject, asking, "How was your class?"

"It was long!" Stephen let out a sigh, "but I've learned a lot already. Professor Chapman had so many great stories about the Revolutionary War and how, as a result, things have changed here in the states. Are all the professors that interesting?"

"Doubtful," William and Claudius said in unison.

"Rumor has it there are some real snoozers!" Claudius remarked.

"Well, I'm excited to go to my Mathematics class next," Stephen announced.

CHAPTER 13

DECEMBER 1858: AT THE COLLEGE OF NEW JERSEY, DONning hats, scarves, and gloves, a group of 'Nassaus" prepared to go out into the snowy day. One student was reading the train schedule as the others tied thin orange bandanas around their heads.

If we take this train," Chauncey Field informed, pointing to the schedule, "we'll have time to dispense at least an hour of havoc on those Queensmen before we have to return."

Unanimously, the twelve gents from The College of New Jersey agreed. Once on the train destined for New Brunswick, the men continued to plot their attack.

After the nineteen-mile ride north, the men detrained. After a stop in Northropes tavern. They went directly to Rutgers campus where they confronted three unknowing freshmen. Several Nassau's pushed the freshmen against the wall of Hertzog Hall. Reminiscent of a firing line, the remaining men gleefully pelted snowballs at them. Though the freshmen struggled and strained, they were outnumbered and overpowered.

Unable to move, between hits the three shouted, "Help! Help! The Nassaus have us cornered in! Somebody help us!"

Hearing the ruckus, the Queensmen inside Hertzog Hall ran to their windows. Viewing the attack, Stephen, Claudius, William, and others quickly ran to rescue their classmates. Without coats or gloves, it took no time for the men of Hertzog Hall to 'return fire,' pelting snowballs back at the Nassau's. The Nassaus got several more 'shots' in before running off to catch their train home.

Perfectly timed, the Nassaus were invigorated by their stunt. They laughed and hollered as they boarded the train for the return trip to Princeton. Slapping each other on the back, they congratulated each other on a job well done.

"You fellas okay" Claudius asked the three.

One man stood looking at the broken eyeglasses in his hand, shaking his head.

"You should have taken 'em off," Claudius commented wryly.

There was no time for that," replied the distressed man. "We were minding our own business, enjoying the quiet beauty of the snow, when they asked us if we knew the snowmen to our south. We didn't know what they were talking about and figured they had probably come from the tavern. Next thing we knew, they had us up against the wall, outnumbered four to one, and they began pummeling us with the hardest snowballs we've ever known."

"Bastards," Claudius said, looking in the direction they ran. "No worries, we'll go to Princeton to get even, soon. Maybe we'll find that southern belle, eh Gano?"

Not recognizing the sinister tone in Claudius' comment, Stephen replied, "She'll need no introduction. She's a beauty. But these Princeton men, I'm starting to really dislike them!"

Smiling, Claudius repeated, "Mark my words, we'll get even with those bastards real soon and paint that cannon red."

"Why paint the cannon red. Stephen questioned. You will find out in due time Claudius replies.

Next Saturday we'll have to stick around to study, but the one after that, we'll go then. We'll take the owl."

"You know I'll be there!" Stephen confirmed.

"I'm counting on you, Gano! Let's spread the word," Claudius encouraged.

CHAPTER 14

STEPHEN WAS WATCHING AS THE COUNTRYSIDE PASSED BY the train window. He was deep in thought about the task ahead. He had no idea what the five men should expect when they got into Princeton. Their mission was clear, however. Get to the cannon unseen.

"PRINCETON JUNCTION; STOP, TRENTON next," shouted the conductor, startling Stephen from his daydreams.

Getting off the mainline, the Queensmen transferred to the relatively new Princeton Shuttle train (the Dinky) that would take them 2.7 miles to The College of New Jersey campus. During the eight-minute ride, the men discussed the final details of their plan. In addition, Claudius enlightened the others about some Princeton history.

"Did you know that Old Nassau was almost named 'Belcher Hall' after the then Governor of New Jersey?" Claudius informed. "He donated a huge sum of money and was the man responsible for the building being built. When they wanted to name it after him, though, he objected. Instead he wanted it named 'Nassau Hall' to honor his highly regarded 'King William the third....of the illustrious House of Nassau.' Can you imagine if it was called Belcher Hall? We would be calling these lads 'The Belcher Boys' instead of 'The Men of Nassau'."

The five laughed heartily at the thought.

Claudius continued, "But seriously, another interesting piece of history, Princeton was our nation's provisional capital for a short time in the last century. Old Nassau served as the capital building being the seat of the government for several months during a time when there was mutiny in Philadelphia, our country's first capital city. Four hundred Continental soldiers took over the city's munitions depot in an effort to gain back wages owed to them from the Revolution." Also during the Revolutionary war 3 cannon balls were fired at the building by Alexander Hamilton, with 1 hitting the building wall and one going through a window decapitated King George's portrait. I heard recently that each graduating class is going to plant a sprig of ivy that will grow its way up the side of the building wall. So one day in the future this whole wall will be covered in ivy.

The men were impressed with the history lesson their classmate offered. As the Dinky came into Princeton they could see a bunch of boys playing on a pond, a local hockey-like game called "shinny." Coming to a full stop on the Princeton campus, however, their attention turned to revenge. They exited the train with resolve.

As it was their first trip to Princeton that year, the Queensmen had agreed they would move across campus quickly and get acquainted with the town before executing their plan. Wandering around town, they were impressed by the architecture of the buildings they viewed. Passing the "Nassau Inn," the town tavern, they made sure to stay well out of sight. Walking down Witherspoon Street named after John Witherspoon, one of 56 people to sign the Declaration of Independence, the Queensmen were on their way.

Eager to exact their revenge and satisfied with their overview of Princeton, the men headed back to the campus. There were several boys playing handball against the wall of the great Nassau Hall. Nonchalantly walking to the back of the building, they found their target: the end of the sunken cemented black cannon sticking out of the ground.

Looking from one to the next, the men nodded in agreement that it was time. Jacob slid a small paint can out from under his overcoat. With the speed of lightning, he covered the previously black cannon with the dark red paint.

Having succeeded in executing their objective, the five men quickly left the scene, pretending nothing had happened. They walked, casually, back toward the town.

Resuming typical banter, Jacob asked Stephen, "Any sign of your southern beauty? Brunette, blue eyed, and well built if I remember your description correctly?"

"Yeah, that's right," Stephen replied. " And no, I haven't seen her yet, but the day's not over."

Walking down Nassau Street, the Queensmen spotted a group of cane carrying well-dressed men talking with three young beautiful women in front of the Bainbridge House. Dressed in long, colorful, oval hoop skirts, the women captivated the young men.

As they got closer, John Van Nest questioned Stephen, "Is that her, Gano? Stephen shaking his head yes. She sure is pretty. John stuttered excitedly.

The Nassau men were speaking poetry and singing to the women, strutting like peacocks for their attention. As the Queensmen watched, Claudius asked, "Do you think we can edge in on those guys and meet your lady friend?"

Daniel agreed, "Those jammie bits of jam sure are well guarded, Gano. You are one lucky guy to have met her on an empty train or you probably wouldn't have had a chance! A woman who looks like that should never travel alone!"

"Make no mistake about it, gentlemen. Despite that pretty exterior, Marianne Glen can take care of herself," Stephen assured them.

"No mistaking here, Gano," Daniel responded, "she sure is quite the gal."

Claudius patted Stephen on the back and complimented, "Gano, you're a man of true honor. That you will stay faithful to a girlfriend back in England when you have access to that bombshell, well, let's just say I don't know if I could stand up to the temptation. Your lady back home must be very special."

Casting his gaze downward, Stephen said humbly, "She is. I've known her ever since I was a wee tyke. I told her I'd come back to her and I will keep my word."

Well, looking at your North Carolina peach, you sure are gonna need a lot of willpower!" Daniel warned.

"What doesn't kill me will make me stronger," Stephen answered stoically. "But I'm really not tempted. She's a nice girl, that's all."

Staring at Marianne, Claudius chimed in, "Then friend, you're gonna soon look like Hercules!"

After the laughter subsided, Claudius asked, "How about an introduction?"

Cautiously, Stephen began to walk toward Marianne and her entourage. Turning to his mates, he mumbled, "She probably won't even recognize me. It's been a couple of months since we met on the train. Besides, she's probably being courted by one of those Nassau's singing to her."

"Yeah, you're probably right," agreed Claudius.

As the men neared the gathering of the students, Stephen heard his name, "Is that you Stephen Gano?"

Surprised and acting like it was the first time he'd seen her, Stephen looked at her and called, "Marianne?"

"Well come on over here. Were you gonna just walk by me and not say hello?" Marianne questioned. "Let me introduce you to my girlfriends."

The Queensmen eagerly approached the women. They nearly fell over themselves jockeying to get close. But the men attending the women were none too pleased. They stepped forward with their canes gripped firmly.

"Stephen," Marianne started, "these are my friends, Teresa and Barbara."

As the Queensmen moved toward the women in an effort to properly greet them, the Nassaus used their bodies and canes to block contact. One man warned, "These Queens are out of their kingdom and are looking to steal our princesses. I don't think that's a wise move."

Another demanded, "We don't need your kind here! Find a woman in your own neck of the woods. These girls are Princetonians and will have nothing to do with the likes of you. Go back from whence you came, now!"

Defensively, Claudius replied, "These women deserve a whole lot more than the likes of you fellows! Why don't we let these fine young ladies decide? We've been summoned and would appreciate you moving out of our way so we can properly greet them."

"Are all you boys working-class foreigners? bullied a Nassau. "Get out of here before we have to forcibly remove you!"

Claudius, holding his temper, replied, "Dear sirs, we most certainly heard you, and we understood every word you spoke. I don't believe you heard me. Unless these lovely ladies ask us to leave, we will not be moving one square inch away. We've been summoned. Now move aside and let us offer a proper greeting."

The women giggled as they watched the men vie for their attention.

Looking to one another, and then to the girls, the Nassaus were prepared to fight. Fortunately, Marianne interjected, "Now boys, you're being way too protective. This man is my friend, and I've invited him and his friends to meet Teresa, Barbara and myself. You're acting like bullies and I'll have none of it, so stand down if you'd like to have anything to do with us in the future."

The men looked at one another sheepishly and nodded. They didn't want to risk losing access to Marianne or her friends. Puffing out their chests in a final show of strength, they moved aside.

One by one, the men shook hands with the ladies. Claudius, with all his bravado, kissed the back of each hand. As the Queensmen began to make small talk with the women, they heard a faint whistle. Realizing the dinky was preparing to leave the station, they knew they had to run for it. It was the last train of the day.

Quickly saying their goodbyes and making their excuses, the men turned and ran as fast as they could.

"I hope to see you and your friends again soon," Stephen shouted as he ran behind his mates.

They got to the train with no time to spare. Out of breath, the men quickly found seats.

CHAPTER 15

THE SEMESTER WAS COMING TO A HOLIDAY BREAK. IT WAS Sunday. After church, the men of Rutgers College dispersed to enjoy their "free" time. Some walked the grounds, some read, some practiced bowling on the outdoor lane. Behind Olde Queens Hall, Stephen Gano was involved in a kicking contest. The men had made a makeshift goal out of wooden posts and hung a rope across them. With ample field to run and kick, they challenged one another to move further and further from the goal each time they attempted to kick a ball over.

As the boys competed, the young athletic enthusiast, Reverend Chester D. Hartranft looked on. He was a seminarian with great interest in sports. Sometimes he participated, but this time he just watched with enthusiasm, shouting encouragement as the competition wore on.

Joining Reverend Hartranft, William Leggett said, "Looks like Gano is winning again!"

"That it does," the Reverend replied. "He's not just fast and strong, he's precise too! Look at how his kicks go seamlessly over the goal every time."

After his last kick, seeing Legget and Hartranft chatting, Stephen walked over to join them. Greetings turned to compliments as the men gushed over Stephen's talent with the ball.

Humbly, Stephen explained, "Kicking the ball has always been my favorite part of the game. My father taught me how to kick straight and long. He used to say, "why make the effort to miss the opportunity." I practiced with my father often."

Taking a moment to gather his emotions, Stephen continued, "Kicking the ball over the goal is a lot less damaging then running it through a maul of men."

Nodding their heads, both men agreed fully.

After a moment of silence, William said, "Hey, Gano, you're an outstanding athlete for sure! So the gang and I are planning to challenge the Princeton Nine to a baseball game in the Spring. Are you interested in joining us?"

"The Princeton Nine?" Stephen asked.

"Yeah, the Princeton Nine, the Nassau's baseball team. Have you heard of them?" William queried.

"Yeah, I have, actually. On the train, when I met Marianne, she told me her brother played for that team. She explained all about it," Stephen remembered.

"Did she tell you they're the best team around these parts? Undefeated for years!" William declared.

"She did tell me that, and she said her brother is one of their best players. She told me he was a Greyback Confederate soldier in the Civil War, too," Stephen remarked.

William asked, "Well, what do you think ? Will you help us out?"

Thinking about it, Stephen remembered his promise to his mother. This was baseball though, not a brutal game, not football, and he had only promised to stay away from football.

"Sure," Stephen confirmed, "but I've never played baseball before."

"Great!" William exclaimed. "We'll start practicing in early Spring. With your athletic prowess, you'll pick it up in no time! If we could defeat the 'nine,' we might be able to gain back a bit of our honor."

"What do you mean our honor?" Stephen questioned.

"I'll have to give you some more history between the two schools to explain," William offered. "It started with the canon wars. We had in our possession a thousand-pound 'Revolutionary War' cannon that George Washington left behind that was used in the 'Battle of New Brunswick.' In 1838 we got news that the 'Princeton Blues,' a local militia company composed of Nassaus and others, were going to try to steal it. Despite the tip off, we weren't able to stop them. Somehow the brilliant bastards pulled off a very well planned caper. To this day we don't know how they did it! We made sure to watch all the roadways but somehow, they got it passed us.

"Once they had it, they sunk it into ten feet of cement, ensuring we couldn't steal it back. That's why we painted it red the other day. We can't steal it back, but we can remind the Nassaus that it's still ours!"

"Wow, I'm beginning to understand this rivalry very clearly now!" Stephen responded.

"Yeah! They took a smaller cannon from us too, but that big one was the one we were really protecting. When they cemented that big 'ol cannon behind Old Nassau Hall, they cemented their superiority over us. That big one is the one that hurts the most. Queensmen have been painting it red every chance we get since."

CHAPTER 16

SPRING TIME 1869. FLOWERS WERE BLOOMING ON CAMPUS and many students were out enjoying the spring weather. Stephen and his cohorts were practicing for the baseball game. Throwing and catching the ball, hitting and running, the men were determined to put forth a good effort against the Princeton Nine.

Following practice, the Queensmen huddled to discuss their strengths and weaknesses, strategizing how to win the upcoming game.

"How're you taking to baseball, Gano?" William queried.

"I really enjoy hitting the cowhide off the ball," Stephen joked.

"We could still use a few more players," William fretted. Chester Harris said he'd play, but he hasn't shown up to practice. He's a good pitcher. We don't have much time left before the game next week."

It was a sunny day and the birds were singing in the breeze. The eight would-be Rutgers baseball players assembled behind Olde Queens Hall. The sound of a newly minted lawnmower resonated in the air as a worker walked back and forth, pushing the revolving blade over the grass.

Reverend Hartranft arrived with a horse drawn carriage. He had arranged to help transport the men to Princeton where the game would be played. Despite the three-hour ride ahead of them, the men were enthusiastic and eager. Five loaded in with their Reverend, while the remaining three men followed on horseback.

In the carriage, the men discussed the newly constructed railway that now connected both sides of this great United States, the opportunity it would bring and the golden spike that was driven in to celebrate this great achievement, then the conversation quickly moved onto the game they were about to play. "Ok, men, let's review our positions and what we need to do to beat the Nassaus," Claudius suggested.

"I'm taking infield," Stephen offered.

"Good Gano, put yourself in at short field. I'll take first base," William said.

"Okay Leggett," Claudius approved. "I'll take pitcher."

"Yeah Rockefeller, that's where you belong. Since we don't have Harris, you have the best arm," William agreed.

With the positions sorted out, the team discussed tactics. Knowing the nine were "murderous with the lumber," when in the field, the Queensmen would have to stay alert and ready to catch the ball at all times.

The Princeton Nine were already practicing as the Queensmen approached. "Princeton 9" was embroidered in black on the backs of their dark orange shirts. Without special "uniforms," the Rutgers team felt immediately intimidated. Watching the nine's well organized warm up, the mood became even more apprehensive. The men knew they were in for a real contest. Slowly, they walked onto the field.

With intention to be overheard, Marianne's brother, "Tar Heel", commented, "Well, look at that, they dared to show up."

William responded, "We are men of our word!" Then, attempting to counter the intimidation he felt, he pronounced, "And I give you my word, we will give you all you can handle in this baseball game.!"

As the snickering subsided, the team captains, William Leggett and Bill Gummere, shook hands. Gummere offered the field to Rutgers for warm-up. Graciously, Leggett accepted.

With the Rutgers men assembled on the field, Gummere noticed only eight men to Princeton's nine. "Hey, Leggett," Gummere called, "You down a man?"

"Unfortunately, yes," Leggett responded.

"I'll even it up and take one of my guys out. I wouldn't want you to say we won because of an unfair advantage," Gummere chuckled.

William responded no need for that we had enough time and fair warning to field a full squad. A few just did not show.

After warming up, the Queensmen moved off the field. Looking around, Claudius spotted Marianne sitting at the sideline.

"Hey, Gano, isn't that your queen over there?" Claudius baited.

"My queen is in England. What are you talking about?" Stephen asked.

"Your southern belle, Marianne," Claudius said, pointing.

As soon as Marianne saw Stephen looking in her direction, she began waving wildly. She got up and headed toward him, much to the chagrin of the Princeton Nine.

A bit surprised, Stephen greeted, "Well hello Miss Marianne Glen!"

The rest of the team watched with envy as Marianne fussed over Stephen.

"Is your brother playing today?" Stephen asked.

Observing his sister's location, furiously, "Tar Heel" marched toward Marianne. Grabbing her by the arm, he attempted to pull her away. "We don't talk to the enemy!" "Tar Heel" reprimanded.

Smiling and pretending not to notice her brother's hard grip on her arm, Marianne said, "Tar Heel", this is Stephen. You remember me telling you about the gentleman I met on the train home from New York, don't you?"

Putting himself between Marianne and Stephen, as if he hadn't heard her at all, "Tar Heel" repeated, "No talking to the enemy!"

Embarrassed and agitated, Marianne dutifully went with her brother. She looked back at Stephen as if to say she was sorry.

"Who was that menace, Gano?" Jacob asked. "Was it her boyfriend?"

"No it was her brother," Stephen answered. "He's supposed to be one of the best players on the Princeton team."

Having discussed final details for the game, the captains returned to their teams. The Queensmen would bat first.

"Ready boys?" William Leggett asked. "We're at home plate first. Grab some lumber and get ready to smash that cowhide!"

Stephen was the first up to bat. Having never hit in a real game, he was a tad nervous, but he didn't disappoint. As the pitcher reared back and the ball sped toward him, Stephen swung with the same precision he used when kicking a ball.

Her brother's anger didn't deter Marianne from cheering for Stephen as the ball shot up high and well beyond the outfielders. She was on her feet, screaming, as Stephen Gano ran around the bases: first, second, third, HOME RUN!

The Queensmen had wondered if they had a chance at winning against the infamous Princeton Nine. With Stephen's early home run, the Rutgers team was encouraged. Unfortunately, their optimism was short-lived. They quickly got 3 outs then it was the Nine's turn at the lumber. The Nassaus brutalized the cowhide over and over again hitting long far home runs, revealing in short order the inexperience of the Rutgers Squad. In a humiliating defeat, the Princeton Nine took the game, 40 to 2.

As was the tradition, the teams shook hands following the final out. After walking the line, Bill Gummere suggested, "Hey, fellas, no hard feelings. After all, you were down a man." He laughed as he said it, then continued, "Stay for a bonfire and supper?"

"Thanks for the offer," William replied. "We need to get back to campus. Some other time."

Heads hung low, the Queensmen began to walk toward their wagons and horses. William Leggett turned and shouted, "Gummere!"

"Yeah?" Bill answered.

"Now that you whooped us on the diamond," William began, "how about giving us a chance to win back some honor in a football game this upcoming fall?"

"Tar Heel" interjected, "Whooped you? It was a diamond disaster!"

The Princeton Nine roared with laughter. "Tar Heel" continued, "We'll defeat you in any endeavor, just like we defeated you today and in the cannon wars."

Ignoring "Tar Heel'" jabs, William Legget informed, "We'll send a formal challenge, then."

Piling into the wagon and on their horses, the Queensmen left for New Brunswick, defeated and demoralized. As they rode away, one of the Nassaus yelled "Maybe you can find the missing cannon on your way back to New Brunswick." Laughter echoed in their ears.

"At least we can count on you to whoop 'em in football, Gano!" William said. "Hands down you're a better footballer than any of them!"

"I'm not going to play in the football game, Leggett," Stephen confessed.

Pretending not to hear him, the team moved onto a less difficult subject.

"I know why we played so badly," Claudius announced.

"Why is that?" Jacob inquired.

"Because our eyes were on Stephen's southern belle's peaches instead of the cowhide!" Claudius bellowed, erupting in laughter.

Stepping into the banter, Jacob added, "I thought they were melons!"

Stephen cut into the dense laughter with a serious tone, "She's not mine, gentlemen."

Ignoring Stephen's tone, Claudius insisted, "You need to get us more time with her, in that case!"

"I will, I will," Stephen insisted. "It's not like there's been a whole lot of opportunity, with the Princeton men and her brother hovering around her."

"Too bad she had to see us get slaughtered by her brother's team!" Jacob commented.

The team nodded in agreement.

CHAPTER 17

IT WAS A HOT JUNE DAY IN PRINCETON WHEN A STUDENT
messenger knocked on the large, wooden door of the College of New Jersey
dormitory, "East College." Upon opening the door, Bill Gummere was presented with an envelope. Returning to the gathering room, he cracked the
seal, took out the paper, and began to read.

"Well, well," Bill announced, "once again those Queensmen kept their
word." Pointing to one of his friends, he ordered, "Go get the others."

"What do you have there," Big Mike asked. Gummere's roommate was
a goliath of a man, and just as smart.

"I'll read it as soon as we're all here," Bill answered.

One by one, men arrived at the gathering room to hear the news. Finally,
Bill read:

> *To the men of Nassau:*
>
> *The Queensmen of Rutgers College do hereby challenge you to a series
> of three football games as follows:*
>
> *Game 1: to be played on Commons Field, Sicard Street, New
> Brunswick, New Jersey on November 6, 1869 at 3pm.*
>
> *Game 2: to be played on a field chosen by the men of Nassau,
> Princeton, New Jersey, November 13, 1869.*
>
> *Game 3: to be played, if necessary, on Commons Field at Sicard
> Street, New Brunswick, New Jersey on November 20, 1869*

We will use the London Football Association 1863 Rules as a guide. Final rules of play to be determined by team captains at the beginning of each game.

Your kind reply should be made within two weeks of the date of receipt. Shy of such a reply, we will assume you have forfeited.

Sincerely,

William Leggett, Captain The Queensmen of Rutgers College

Preston, a loud fellow, bellowed, "Forfeit? We'll cream 'em. We whooped 'em on the diamond and we'll whoop 'em on the green! We will thump them with any rules they choose! Just like we did to the Princeton Theological Seminary last year

"Bring on Big Mike, and Colonel Weir and his boys. I'm sure there's a long list of men who'd like to beat up those chumps!"

The room erupted in laughter.

Chauncy Field, a tall, handsome fellow whose family helped in the founding of Rhode Island, added, "We'll be able to destroy those Queensmen legally! Or should I say women?"

After the laughter subsided, Chauncy continued, "Do you think they'll wear their skirts?"

More laughter erupted as Chauncy strolled across the floor, pretending to be wearing a dress and high heels.

"Well boys," Bill queried, "are we on for a bit of football? Shall we show them, once and for all, who's superior?"

Confirmation was loud and unanimous.

CHAPTER 18

IT WAS A HOT JULY DAY. ON THE SECOND FLOOR OF Hertzog Hall, several students including Stephen were busy tapping metal keys on a metal box, causing metal arms to rise, thereby thrusting ink cloth against paper. The sequence produced letters on the paper, potentially making words, then sentences, then paragraphs.

Claudius and Jacob burst through the door and asked, "What's that you have there, Stephen?"

Stephen explained that he and several others were asked to try out the new fangled machines. "A 'type write'," Stephen said, "given to the school to put through its paces. If it passes, John Sholes will patent it!"

Stephen continued banging on the keys with increasing speed. His initial word of choice was "RUTGERS," and he typed it repeatedly: RUTGERS RUTGERS RUTGERS RUTGERS RUTGERS RUTGERS RUTGETS

"Oops," Stephen shrugged. "The only downside to this contraption is if I hit the wrong key, I can't really change it on the paper. Plus, the keys stick sometimes, especially the faster I go, but maybe that's correctable."

Switching gears, Stephen began typing SHUT THE NASSAUS UP, SHUT THE NASSAUS UP, SHUT THE NASSAUS UP, trying to go faster each time.

"Careful now, Gano," Claudius warned. "Don't wear it out!"

"The professor said to put it through its paces," Stephen defended. "I'm doing my best to do just that!"

Tired of playing with the "type write," Stephen got up from his desk and headed for the door.

"What's it called again?" Jacob asked.

"A 'type write'," Stephen responded.

Walking into the room with an envelope in his hand, Preston announced, "A messenger just brought this. It's from the boys of Nassau. Shall I open it?"

"Let me have it," William said, quickly grabbing the envelope out of Preston's hand. He wasted no time tearing it open. Pulling out the letter, he read:

We, the men of Nassau, with William Gummere as our captain, enthusiastically accept the Queensmen's football challenge. We fully consent to a best two out of three game series.

We hereby request that fair catch and free kick be allowed in all games. Captains will finalize all the games' knotty points of play prior to kick off.

Sincerely,
Captain William Gummere
The Winning Men of Nassau

Claudius was the first to speak, "So, we got what we asked for."

"What's 'fair catch' and 'free kick'," Jacob queried. Recognizing the level of inexperience, Stephen shook his head. He knew these men were going to get slaughtered on the field.

William answered Jacob's question, "It means if the ball is in the air, you can call off a collision and freely attempt to catch, then put the ball on the ground for a free kick. The defense has to also yield ten paces."

Stephen chimed in, "If I were captain, I wouldn't accept their fair catch, free kick request. Based on what I saw at our baseball catastrophe, they're bigger and taller than us. It would give them an unfair advantage."

"You know a lot about the game, Stephen," William praised. "Why is it you aren't going to join us in our quest?"

"I just can't," Stephen replied, looking down at his feet.

"Well," William asserted, "with or without you, we have to assemble a winning team. I'm tired of living with the shame of being the losing school. I'm tired of them having bragging rights. We're better than them and we need to prove it. We have to show those Nassaus what we're made of. This time, we have to reign victorious!"

The men in the room snickered.

"Boys, laugh if you will, but this is a serious affair!" William continued. "Who wants to defeat those haughty, cocky guys once and for all? We have to smash the arrogant prep boys of Nassau and show them who's better. The sooner we can get a team together, the more time we'll have to practice!"

Desperately wanting to participate, Stephen offered, "I'll help in any way I can. I was a pretty good player back in Rugby, and I grew up watching my father play. He was a legend where I come from. I can provide guidance and strategies."

William replied, "I don't understand why you won't play with us, Gano, but if the best we can get from you is guidance, I guess we'll take it."

"Let's start by asking the biggest and strongest to join us," Stephen directed. "And add the smartest. Brains and brawn will go a long way in this game. Let's see who we can find here at Rutgers, and look in the New Brunswick area as well."

"I'll get right on it," Claudius offered, adding, "I know a few guys who might join us, but they're not local."

"Who are you thinking about, Claude?" William prodded.

"For one, 'Mad Dog' Madison Ball," Claudius said. "He fought in the Civil War. He attended Rutgers a few years back; he is probably 26-27 years old now. Not only is he a strong guy, but he's said to be doggone crazy, too. I'm sure he'd love to take out some frustrations on the men of Nassau.! Then there's Henry Steele. I'm hoping his name fits. I heard he has a history of footballing. He was here a few years back also. Neither one of them graduated yet." Plus I know George Large will play, he is one of the smartest, toughest and fearless men around.

"No doubt the men of Nassau team will include Big Mike, a giant freight train of a man and the raw-boned Kentuckian Colonel Weir, another Grayback. I heard Colonel Weir still doesn't believe the war is over. He's probably got a group of war buddies who'll play as well and try to make ducks and drakes out of us," William commented. "If they play football the way they play baseball, we'll have quite a force to contend with. How are you going to find Mad Dog and Henry Steele?"

Thinking about it for a moment, Claudius replied, "Steele works with his father in Barnegat Bay, near the lighthouse. He's a shoreline fisherman and clam digger. Mad Dog, well last I heard he was working in the bogs south of Cranbury."

"Might take some effort to find your men," William cautioned Claudius, "but we'll need all the help we can get, so go get 'em!"

"I'd love to see the famous 'Jersey Shore Line'," Stephen said. "I'll go with you, Claudius. How are you figuring we'll get there?"

Considering his options, Claudius replied, "I'll ask the Reverend if we can borrow a couple of his horses. Can you ride Stephen?

"Of course I can," Stephen replied, almost insulted by the question.

"Asking Reverend Hartranft is a great idea," William encouraged. "I'm sure he wants us to beat the Nassaus as much as we do. He'll no doubt help in any way he can."

"For sure," Claudius agreed. "If he could play in the game, I'm sure he'd do that too!"

"I'll get busy posting signs around campus. I'll post some at the train station, too," William offered. "How does this sound? "Footballers wanted in a quest to defeat the Men of Nassau." I'm sure there are a few neighbors who would give a tooth or a broken finger to shut down the bravado of those Princetonians!"

Eager to secure the best men, Claudius and Stephen immediately set about acquiring horses from the good Reverend. Living in a stone farmhouse not far from campus, Reverend Hartranft was home for the evening. In the summer heat, the boys walked a few blocks and knocked on his door. No one answered.

Not wanting to leave without completing their mission, the boys walked around to the back of the house. Searching the landscape, they spotted Reverend Hartranft on his knees in the middle of a massive vegetable garden.

Trying not to startle the man by getting too close, Claudius called his name, "Reverend Hartranft?"

Startled nonetheless, the Reverend moved quickly from his gardening posture to upright. Spotting Claudius and Stephen, the Reverend composed himself and asked, "Yes, boys?"

Aware that they had disturbed the Reverend in his private time, Claudius and Stephen apologized profusely.

"Not to worry," Reverend Hartranft reassured, "What brings you to my home this evening?"

Claudius spoke first, "We know you are as proud to be a part of Rutgers College as we are, sir. Remember the baseball game we played against The College of New Jersey a few months ago?"

"Sadly, I can't forget," the Reverend acknowledged. "We had our fannies whooped. And now those Nassau men think they're even better than they thought before!"

"Exactly," Stephen chimed in.

"So we formally challenged them to a series of three football games, and they accepted," Claudius blurted out. "Now we need to assemble a team that can actually beat them. I know of two men who I think would be great assets, 'Mad Dog' Madison Ball and Henry Steele."

"Football against the men of Nassau?" Reverend Hartranft exclaimed. "I love a good football game! But the faculty at large does not. With the exception of an occasional annual one day brawl between the incoming freshmen and the upperclassmen, football is prohibited. Ball and Steele are very good choices. I'll see what I can do to help you out."

With a wink, the Reverend got back on his knees, returning to his gardening.

"Uh, Reverend Hartranft?" Stephen persisted.

"Yes, Stephen, what is it?" replied the Reverend.

"We came to ask you for horses," Stephen informed. "You see, Mad Dog and Henry Steele no longer live here in New Brunswick. In order to ask for their help in the games, we have to find them. Claudius thinks one is in Barnegat and the other south of Cranbury. We were wondering if we could borrow two horses this weekend, so we can look for them?"

"Ah," said Reverend Hartranft, "of course. You realize that journey will take you a full day each way?"

"Yes, sir," the boys answered.

"Very well then, I'll have two of my finest saddled up and ready," Reverend Hartranft confirmed. "Meet me at the stables on Saturday morning, 6:00 a.m. sharp."

"Thank you, sir, we'll see you on Saturday," Claudius agreed.

As the boys walked away, the Reverend called, "When you get back, we'll talk about strategies. I'm going to do everything in my power to help you win our honor back!"

"Thank you, sir," the boys replied.

"You're most welcome," the Reverend responded. "And rest assured, I'll also be looking for players who can help us insure a win."

CHAPTER 19

AT 6:00 A.M., CLAUDIUS AND STEPHEN ARRIVED AT REVEREND Hartranft's farmhouse. They found the Reverend ready and waiting, standing by the stable with maps and supplies.

"Good morning!" Reverend Hartranft greeted. "The horses are ready, how are you?"

Yawning, the boys assured the Reverend they were ready and eager to depart. Reverend Hartranft provided each of them with a bundle containing several biscuits, dried meats, and assorted vegetables and fruits. He showed them the maps and underscored the routes they should take, avoiding rivers and difficult terrain.

Claudius and Stephen tried to show their abundant appreciation. Their words fell short.

"I'm happy to help, gentlemen. I'll do whatever it takes to defeat those gloating Princetonians!" the Reverend declared. "I'll even order a new rubber football for the match. It's amazing how far they've come from the old pig bladder type."

Mounting the horses, Stephen and Claudius took a few minutes to reacquaint themselves with riding. Comfortable, they bid farewell to the Reverend, assuring him they would return the next evening.

Nodding, the Reverend confirmed, "I'll see you back here tomorrow by dusk. Godspeed."

Tipping their hats, Claudius and Stephen rode off. Before they were out of range, Reverend Hartranft shouted, "Remember, look for the lighthouse, you can't miss it!"

After riding many hours it was late afternoon, Stephen shouted, "Wow, there it is Claudius, there's the lighthouse!"

Above the horizon they could see Barnegat Lighthouse piercing the clear blue sky. Accelerating their pace, it wasn't long before they could see water.

"There's the Atlantic Ocean!" Stephen declared. "It's so different from this vantage point. When I rode across on the steamship, it seemed endless."

Claudius corrected, "That's not the ocean that's the Barnegat Bay. The Atlantic is on the other side of that barrier island. It is magnificent, and fun to swim in as well. But there's no time for that now. Let's hope we can find Henry Steele, and that he accepts our invitation."

"He'll be here," Stephen assured. "I can feel it in my bones."

Using the lighthouse as their guide, the boys rode to the huge bay. It was low tide and there were dozens of men and boats scattered along the bay shoreline. They saw various fishing lines originating from the land or strewn from the boats, and men were knee deep in the water, using their rakes and or feet to dig up clams. Further out, the men were pulling in their metal traps, hoping to have caught the prized giant blue-clawed crabs.

Walking toward a group of fishermen, Stephen asked, "Does anyone know Henry Steele?"

In unison, the men pointed south. "He's down a ways," said one.

"Look for the boat with the red stripe on it. You'll find him on or near it," shared another.

Thanking the men, the boys headed south. As they approached the red striped wooden boat, they called out, "Henry Steele?"

Looking up from the water, Henry Steele spotted the two young men on their horses. Rising from the deck, he called, "Yeah, who's looking?"

Claudius and Stephen rode closer and said, "We are Queensmen, here to ask a noble favor."

"Queensmen, eh?" Henry said, washing his hands off in the bay and walking toward the boys. "What sort of favor?"

Henry Steele was not a large man, as it turned out, at least not in stature. But he was built like a brick shithouse, and that was the kind of muscle the Queensmen needed to help win the game!

"The sort of favor that would put those darned Nassaus right in their place," Claudius said as he and Stephen dismounted their horses.

Stephen explained, "We're students at Rutgers College. We understand you attended a few years ago. We thought you might be interested in an opportunity. We've been looking for a way to win back our honor from the Nassaus. They always think they're better than us after their "cannon war" caper. Their constant gloating is always over the top. We tried to get even in a baseball challenge recently, but we lost by a landslide. It was horrible leaving the baseball diamond as they snickered and taunted us. We left with our proverbial tails between our legs. We think we have a better chance with football. The Nassaus have agreed to a best two-out-of-three challenge, beginning in November. We're looking for the best men to join us, and your name came up. What do you think?"

Henry perked up the minute he heard "win our honor back," but when he heard how, he completed the short walk to Stephen and Claudius with a hop in his step! After wiping his hands with a rag he heartily shook each boy's hands, Henry inquired, "When's the first game?"

"November 6," Claudius answered. "Three o'clock. First game will be played on the Rutgers Commons field."

A group of men were cleaning up and preparing to eat part of their catch. Henry invited Stephen and Claudius to join them for supper as they discussed the matter further.

"I'd like nothing better than to plant those prickly preps into the Brunswick sod," Henry declared.

"Is that a yes?" Claudius asked.

"You can count me in!" Henry confirmed. "My father's been after me to resume classes anyway. I never did finish my schooling. Maybe this is just the push I need to get back to Rutgers."

"That's fantastic!" Claudious exclaimed. We'll look forward to your arrival and will be having a "bonfire" Thursday before the game.

Telling the boys he'd make arrangements as soon as possible, Henry Steele asked a variety of questions about classes and campus life. He asked about the pranks the Nassaus were playing.

Eating more than their fill of fresh seafood. Claudius said, "It's great news that you're joining us, Henry! And thank you for the amazing meal! Nothing like fresh caught seafood from the Jersey Shore. We do have to get on our way. There's another gent we'd like to invite to join us for the games and it's a distance back to New Brunswick. We promised the good Reverend we'd be back with his horses tomorrow by sunset."

"Who else are you looking for?" Henry asked.

"'Mad Dog' Madison Ball," Claudius answered.

"Mad Dog," Henry boomed. "He's the quickest man this side of the Delaware! I saw him catch a rabbit once, with nothing but his agility, speed, and bare hands!"

"Yeah," Claudius added, "I've heard about him. That's why we need him to play."

"Thank you for the food. We really have to go if we're to keep our promise to the Reverend," Stephen reiterated. He took out the map Reverend Hartranft had given him and noted the route.

As Claudius and Stephen mounted their horses, Henry proclaimed, "I'll die for dear old Rutgers! Hail to the Colonel!" as he pounded his right fist against his chest, over his heart, twice.

Riding off, the Queensmen smiled. They were one step closer to a win against the Nassaus.

Claudius and Stephen rode until the sun began to set. Dismounting, they offloaded their supplies and set up camp. Stephen gathered wood and Claudius made a fire. By the crackle of their campfire, they lay on the ground looking at the stars, Stephen mused, "I never dreamed of such adventures in America. I'm so proud to be a Queensman!"

The men drifted to sleep. The next morning, waking with the sun, the men knew they had limited time. They quickly packed their supplies and got on their way.

"How will we find him?" Stephen asked.

I suspect we'll have to stop and ask along the way," Claudius remarked. "The good Reverend has circled the areas where cranberries are harvested. We'll head in that direction. We'll find him!"

Stephen and Claudius rode many miles asking anyone they saw if they knew where Madison Ball was. As they approached the town of Cranbury, they could see a smattering of wild bushes with red berries. This marshy land did look like a place where cranberries were grown and harvested.

Riding into town, the Queensmen spotted a tavern, the Cranbury Inn. Upon entry, they found a dimly lit room in which men were drinking beer, playing darts, cards, and unwinding from a full day of work. All heads turned as the young men walked in.

Claudius approached the closest table and asked, "Does anyone know where we can find 'Mad Dog' Madison Ball?"

Hearing his name, Ball jumped to his feet. With a wild look in his eyes, and a threat in his tone, he questioned, "Who's asking'?"

Overwhelmed by their good fortune and trying to quickly diffuse any hostility, Stephen offered, "Mr. Ball, we're students at Rutgers College."

"Queensmen!" Mad Dog held his arms wide as a sign of welcome. "Why are you looking for me?"

After properly introducing themselves, Stephen answered, "We challenged the "Men of Nassau to a football game. We could not stand their boasting for one more day. We need your help."

Shaking his head, Mad Dog complained, "Those boys have been tormenting the Rutgers men for years. The cannon wars really pushed their arrogance over the top. I may not have finished at Rutgers, but I wouldn't mind finishing their gloating."

Mad Dog stopped for a moment to consider his time at Rutgers."

Sitting down, Mad Dog thought about what he had just heard. "Football, huh? That's a brutal game. And you came to ask me to play?"

"Yes, would you help us?" Stephen answered.

"I can't tell you how often those bigheaded jerks ride through this way heading to and from the Jersey Shore. Sometimes they stop here for a bite and a beer. Sometimes I have to be restrained. I want to punch those irritating snobs right in the kisser! Making up stories of a 40-2 whooping on the baseball diamond is their most recent boast." Claudius looks at Stephen. "So any chance to put those bullies in their cribs, well, count me in! Not to mention I love a good football game!

Gentlemen, are you hungry? Drinks are on me"

"Thanks, Mad Dog!" Claudius responded. "Though we'd love to stay for a while, we have to get these horses back to Reverend Hartranft. He's expecting us by sundown. We left early yesterday and went out to Barnegat before coming here. We secured the help of Henry Steele, too. You know him, right?"

"Henry Steele!" Mad Dog shouted with a hefty chuckle, "Why I haven't talked to old Henry in a year or more! It'll be great to pummel those Nassaus with Henry!"

Mad Dog walked out of the tavern with Claudius and Stephen. As Henry Steele had done, Mad Dog clenched his right fist and pounded his chest twice, showing his allegiance to the cause.

"I will die for dear old Rutgers," Mad Dog declared.

The boys thanked him profusely and rode off, headed toward New Brunswick.

It was a particularly hot day. As Stephen and Claudius rode on, their thirst got the best of them. Spotting a roadside farm stand, the men went in that direction to quench their thirst and fill their bellies.

Young men and women were gathered at the stand, eating local game birds, drinking apple cider, and making a ruckus.

"Don't look now, friend, but I think I see your southern belle!" Claudius observed.

"Marianne?" Stephen replied, surprised, "How is that possible? What are the odds?"

Claudius replies "with pure destiny". Smiling over at Stephen.

"It's her alright, sitting at the table with those guys from our ill-fated baseball challenge," Claudius assured, keeping a watchful gaze on the beautiful woman. "There's no missing her with that body! She makes you see double and hopefully think single Stephen! Claudius smiling at his last comment.

As they approached, one of the Nassau's including "Tar Heel" recognized Stephen and Claudius and shouted, "Hey, lookie here, two of our 'Queensmen 8' are headed our way."

Another of the men goaded, "Are you looking for your cannon or one of our home runs, boys?"

Marianne demanded that her companions stop their teasing. She encouraged them, "We can all be friends, can't we? After all, these are our neighbors."

"Not until, once and for all, these queens accept that we reign superior," Marianne's brother, "Tar Heel", commanded.

Despite the hostility, Stephen approached Marianne to say hello. "It's nice to see you again, Marianne," Stephen said gently.

"Nice to see you too, Stephen," Marianne replied. "What are you doing here?"

"Claudius and I rode out to the shore yesterday. We were looking for someone. We're on our way back to Rutgers now," Stephen explained, and then asked, "What are you doing here?

Before Marianne could answer, realizing he'd been rude not to introduce his friend, Stephen said, "Oh, and you remember my friend, Clau..."

"Tar Heel" interrupted, "Well boys, best be on your way. Wouldn't want you to be traveling in the dark. It can get rough around these parts at night.

Thinking about what he said and looking at Stephen, "Tar Heel" added, "Oh yeah, I hear the Englishmen is a real meater".

The Princeton group got up and began walking away. Stephen and Claudius were angry and exhausted. They finished their cider and got back on their horses, ready to go home and plan their strategies. Stephen wondered how "Tar Heel" knew he wasn't going to play.

Chapter 20

The boys arrived at Reverend Hartranft's stables as the sun was beginning to set. They felt good to have accomplished what they set out to do; they secured a commitment to play from two strong men who could help their cause. After returning the horses to the stables, Reverend Hartranft accompanied Stephen and Claudius back to Hertzog Hall. Claudius was still fuming over the roadside encounter with the Nassaus. "I want to shut those loudmouths down!" he raged.

"Me, too," Stephen responded.

"With your experience, you could really help the cause," Claudius encouraged.

"I'm sorry. I told you, I can't play," Stephen reiterated.

"I just don't understand why?" Claudius responded.

Looking up to the heavens, Stephen replied, "I just can't." *Maybe one day I will tell you the details of why.*

"I have no choice but to accept your choice, but it sure would be great if you changed your mind! For now, we'll just have to defeat them without you," Claudius affirmed.

Pleased with Claudius' show of determination, Stephen commented, "That's the spirit! Courage is the first step to victory!"

Walking into the room, William greeted the travelers with enthusiasm and asked the obvious question, "Did you get us the footballers?"

Proudly, Stephen confirmed, "That we did! I think they'll both be a strong addition to our team. One is tough as a barn door, and the other fast as a rabbit."

"That's fantastic!" Jacob praised.

Reverend Hartranft interjected, "William, I hear you're going to captain the team. That's wonderful news. There's no one more experienced or worthy. I purchased a new black rubber football for you to use. It's made from India rubber! It's supposed to be the best there is." If everyone chips in I will give it to you boys to keep and practice with, giving us a small advantage over the Nassaus. All shaking their heads in agreement.

"Great!" said Stephen, looking at the ball. "I wonder if it was made in Rugby". "Well, we will be able to practice with this new ball and get a feel for how it will kick and bounce around the field.."

"What do you mean we?" the Reverend asked. "I thought you weren't playing."

"I'm not," Stephen confirmed, "but I'll be helping with strategies and playing in spirit."

"I'll take that," William acknowledged. "But spirit and strategies alone aren't going to win us this game. We still need to draft more warriors of football. Remember, Colonel Weir still thinks he's fighting the Civil War. I'm certain they have more battle-tested players. That's the force we need to combat!"

Reverend Hartranft added, "Yes, Colonel Weir will be a strong player as will Big Mike be another giant of a nuisance to contend with as well. We need to find more of our own to match up. We need to beat them on every level: be better organized, more determined, and filled with surprises. We know those Princeton boys. They are undoubtedly big, strong, smart, and tough."

Realizing the hour and acknowledging the long trip Claudius and Stephen had just taken, the Reverend took his leave, saying, "You boys look tired. Get some shuteye and sleep well. We'll continue to talk tactics after summer break."

CHAPTER 21

UP ON THE SECOND FLOOR OF HERTZOG HALL, WILLIAM, Stephen, Claudius, Winfield and Jacob discussed the team. It was early September and they were close to having a full twenty-five man squad.

"What's the update on our football team?" William asked.

"Twenty-two commits, seven possibilities, captain," Claudius reported.

"Can we get 'em all to Commons Field on Sicard Street Saturday next?" William asked. "We need to start practicing our kicking, blocking, and running. We need to discuss our strategies and start practicing them till they are flawless."

"Yes, I think that'll be fine," Claudius responded.

"Great! What are we doing to secure those final three?" William asked. "

"We've got a good number of freshmen eager to play," Winfield answered. "They don't have much in the way of skill, but they have a whole lot of passion and enthusiasm. Since they've never played, they don't know how brutally rough it'll be. Like the Reverend said, 'ignorance is bliss.' And I told the upperclassmen to keep their traps shut if the newcomers ask questions."

A week has passed, the sky was clear and the air was cool. Players started to file onto the grassy, tree lined, Sicard Street field early Saturday morning. Along one side of the field was a long wooden fence. Spectators usually gathered on the fence to watch whatever was going on in the field.

Approaching Jacob, William asked, "Did we secure the final three?"

Proudly, Jacob responded, "Indeed we did, cap'n. The good Reverend got two more freshmen to commit, and I recruited another Civil War soldier who was living just outside the city limits."

"Great," William remarked. "That'll bring our tally to twenty-five. I think we should keep looking, though. If someone comes along who can better our chances, we can add them as well ."

"Okay, cap'n," Jacob complied.

Shaking hands as they greeted one another, the team members were making small talk. With a booming voice, William greeted the assembled mass, saying, "It's my honor to captain you fine men as we prepare to defeat the men of Nassau of The College of New Jersey. For those who don't know me, my name is William Leggett. I'm going to make us the best team possible, and we are going to become the best football team this side of the Raritan!"

Pointing to Stephen, he continued, "This fine fellow to my right is Stephen Gano. He will be assisting as we iron out our game strategies and become a team with which to be reckoned with. To my left, as many of you know, is Reverend Hartranft. He too will be helping us to become the best team we can be. Ultimately, we will shut down the Nassaus gloat."

The men erupted in hoots and hollers, slapping each around and nodding in agreement.

"As you know," William continued, "football can be played in many forms, depending on the number of players and home team preferences. Stephen, here, is going to tell you the rules as agreed upon to date."

Clearing his voice, Stephen explained, The rules of the game will be guided by using the London Football Association rules. Meaning this will be a kicking game, so no running with the ball. First the playing field will be marked at 360 feet long and 225 feet wide. Because we are swift, that enormous space will offer us great benefits. Placing ourselves in an organized manner will give us our greatest advantage. Surprising the Nassaus with the flying wedge play will also help us a great deal. It's an interlocking arm play that we will practice.

"We will be a team of twenty-five playing against twenty five. As men are injured, they will exit the field. No replacements will be allowed unless the captains decide otherwise.

"The 'no fair catch and free kick rule' will be used. No throwing or running with the ball. No tripping, no hacking. The ball can be batted or kicked with arms, hands, heads, and legs, and I repeat, the ball cannot be carried off and run with in this game. So practice your kicking.

"Goal posts will be eight paces apart. The ball can only be pushed or kicked through the goal posts for a score. Best of ten games or innings as some say, six scores will win the match. Balls that pass the goal line not through the uprights will be kicked back into play by the side protecting that goal. Balls passing the sideline will be kicked back into play by the team that knocked it out. The spectators usually track down the errant balls, so allow them to and rest a little at that time.

"If there's a foul, the fouling team has to allow the other team a free penalty kick backing up 10 paces to allow for the free kick.

"No holding, but hacking is allowed and I repeat no tripping. The 'three-punch rule' will be in effect. So no fighting or you will be removed from the match.

Metal under armor is prohibited.

"The winner of the first coin toss will choose which goal they want to defend. Winner of the second toss gets 'first buck'. We'll switch sides with each goal scored. Each side will choose one referee and two judges from the student body prior to the game start.

"Final knotty points will be decided by the captains the day of the games. First game is Saturday, November 6. Our neighbors will arrive at ten in the morning and we will provide them with our finest courtesies, interest, intrigue and lunch on the river bank. The game will begin at three o'clock p.m. on this very field. Be ready for battle.

"Any questions?"

Daniel spoke up, "What type of ball are we using?"

Stephen responded, "The good Reverend, here, was kind enough to buy us a brand new black India rubber ball." Did everyone chip in for it?

The Reverend held the round ball high for everyone to see. Commenting to one another, a buzz swept over the group. Many had never seen a rubber ball before, let alone used one.

Cutting into the chatter, Stephen said, "Reverend Hartranft has also developed some plays that will razzle dazzle our opponents. He'll be teaching us those and be working on new strategies. Make sure you ask him questions and pay attention! Now, any other questions for me before we review the strategies?"

Hearing none, Stephen continued, "Okay, listen carefully. We'll use the flying wedge on all bucks we take possession of. We'll ram the ball down with our bulldozers and kick it through or push it through the goalposts. We'll use the following signals to show where we want the ball to go."

Stephen demonstrated the various hand signals for left, right, and center and high and low, and a few for some set plays. He had the men mimic him to help them remember. We will practice all these over the coming weeks.

As we determine the strengths of each man, we'll assign our best kickers to be the captains of the enemy goal. The second best kickers will be in the back of a given skirmish. We need the bulldozers, the bigger, slower, strongest men in the middle with interlocking arms, pushing through as hard as is humanly possible using our wedge play to clear the way for the ball dribblers and fielders around them. Once they've pushed close enough to the goal, we will attempt a kick to score or push one under the cross string. Alternatively, the fielders on the sides can and will kick the ball as it comes out of the skirmish to the captain of the enemy goal for a quick strike to score whenever able. Remember, we must keep the ball moving at all times. We'll use our organization, speed, and agility to tire them out. They'll most likely be taller and bigger than us so keeping the ball close to the ground is imperative!"

Noting that Stephen was done, William stepped in and directed, "Okay men, let's practice! We'll start with calisthenics, followed by two laps around the field."

Once adequately conditioned, the men practiced a lot of wedge plays using their hand signals, and ended the practice with plenty of kicking. After a three-hour practice, the team was exhausted.

Gathering the team at center field, Captain William Leggett addressed the group, "Okay boys, that was a great first practice! Next practice will be next Saturday and every Saturday leading up to the first game. Keep up your enthusiasm and determination!"

"Remember," Leggett continued, "practice on your own as often as possible. Especially your kicking. Be sure to stay out of sight, though. We have some crotchety, old professors who are not happy we're doing this. Behind Hertzog Hall is a good place, or off campus. Focus your mind and thoughts on beating the Nassaus! We are the mighty Queensmen and will regain our honor with a victory!"

With great energy, the men of Rutgers shouted and howled in a show of strength and unity.

While in Princeton, William Gummere met with his team members to discuss the impending game against Rutgers. He began, "I heard the Queensmen have had their first practice."

"Good thing, they'll need all the help they can get," "Tar Heel" commented sarcastically, provoking great laughter.

"We can't let our guard down. We'll need to start practicing as soon as possible. Who has committed to play? How many do we have?"

One of the first men to sign onto the team, Homer spoke up, "Colonel Weir has committed. He'll be a terror on the field! He hasn't yet figured out that the war is over. Big Mike is in, too, and Chauncey Field. That takes us to twenty-four. We need one more."

Gummere responded, "Great! Get working on that twenty-fifth man. Ask around town, do what it takes. Spread the word that there'll be a practice on Saturday, nine o'clock in the morning at Conover Field. We're using the London Football Association rules as a guide. We'll go over them at the field."

Cocky as ever, "Tar Heel" sat back in his chair with a big smile on his face and asked, "Do those princesses really think they have a chance at beating us?"

More serious than ever, Gummere leaned in and responded, "I believe they do, "Tar Heel". You know how that game can make mice of men. We have to make sure we're ready. We have to make this contest final and fatal!" Football brings out the best in men so let's prepare as victors and not take anything for granted.

In a show of solidarity, the men at the table broke into the Apache-like Indian battle cry, shrieking, "YA AYA AYA YA YA AAYAAYAA!" The

Confederate soldiers had used the same rebel yell when going into battle. We will use this Apache call to scare the daylights out of the Rutgers players when we start the match, Colonel Weir stated.

"Remember boys, just like in a real war never underestimate the enemy," Gummere warned. "See everyone at practice, then. Saturday morning, nine sharp."

Chapter 22

THE NEXT SATURDAY IN PRINCETON, THE USUAL SIX A.M.
bell at Whig Hall failed to ring. As men woke and realized the time, they
gathered themselves and woke the others. As quickly as they could, they went
to Morning Prayer and then made their way to Conover Field.

"Which one of you geniuses stole the clapper from the bell?" Bill
Gummere inquired of his players.

Receiving only blank stares, Gummere continued, "You know you'll
have to return it before long, right? Our professors aren't stupid. They'll use
trumpets till it's returned and that'll be even worse!"

Defeated, Francis offered, "I was hoping for an excuse to get a bit more
shuteye without being punished for being late to class. I forgot about the
trumpets. I'll return it under cover of darkness."

The students on the field nodded in agreement.

"Okay," Gummere announced as he surveyed his team, "Most of you
have played in a football game before many in last year's game against the
seminary so let's get down to business. We need to use our size and strength
to our utmost advantage. We should be able to crush the puny Queens with
our bulldozers." remember this is a kicking game, so no running with the ball.

Referring to previous discussions he had had with most of the players,
Gummere said, "Since we've already gone over most of the rules, we'll waste
no time in getting to practice."

The men assembled themselves on the field creating 2 teams. They
practiced their fair catch and free kick. They moved the ball effortlessly
down the field and scored with every attempt. Realizing his oversight, Bill
Gummere called the men together and informed them that there would be

no fair catch or free kick in the coming contest. Dispersing once again, they practiced various kicking, blocking, and catching plays. Colonel Weir, fully engaged, pummeled a team member, leaving the player with a certain bruise on his torso and a bleeding lip. All in all, the players made a good show of it for their first practice.

Concluding, Gummere had a few words to say, "You did well men, very well. A few points: First, remember that the Colonel and Big Mike are our best players. Make sure you are playing with them, not against them. Kicking needs to be fine-tuned. Make sure you find time in your schedule to practice on your own. We'll meet next Saturday for another practice, and each Saturday leading up to the game. Remember, we don't want to leave any doubt about who reigns supreme. We're going to destroy the Queensmen!"

Slapping each other on the back, the men left the field hollering, "We will destroy the Queensmen!"

CHAPTER 23

BACK AT HERTZOG HALL, A STUDENT MESSENGER APPROACHED
Jacob Van Fleet. "Excuse me," he said, "I'm looking for Stephen Gano Jr. Can
you tell me where I might find him?"

Jacob responded, "He lives here; I think he went to the river to fish."

"I'll look for him there," The messenger declared. "Thank you."

Walking over to the Raritan River, the messenger spotted a group of
boys fishing off the bank. The beauty of the river was overwhelming, with
boats moving in either direction.

"Excuse me," the messenger called, "Are any of you Stephen Gano Jr.?"

Suddenly made aware of the man standing behind him, Stephen
answered, "Yes, I'm Stephen. Can I help you?"

"I have an important message from Boston for you," the messenger
stated.

Stephen eagerly accepted the envelope the messenger offered. He
quickly opened it, pulled out a letter, and began to read silently:

To Our Dearest Nephew Stephen,

*It is to our great regret that this letter comes to inform you that
your loving mother took on a very high fever over the last week
and a half. She did not wake up this morning. We are saddened
beyond expression and know this comes as quite a shock. We request
you return to Boston immediately as we make arrangements for
her burial.*

With love and heavy heart,
Uncle Peter and Aunt Sarah

In shock and fighting back tears, Stephen handed the letter to his mates. Working hard to gain composure, barely able to speak, he informed his friends he would be taking the next train out. He asked them to tell the professors of his plans.

With utmost respect and kindness, the boys gathered around Stephen to offer their condolences and help. They accompanied him back to the dorm and helped him pack. They went with him to the train station to see him off. He assured them he'd return in a week. After providing bear hugs to all, Stephen's friends watched as he boarded the train.

In Boston, the weather matched Stephen's mood. Exiting the train in the rain, he made his way to his Uncle's carriage. Getting in, he hugged his uncle. Few words were exchanged.

At Uncle Peter's home, Stephen somberly greeted his sisters and aunt. Morgan and Carly Ann burst into tears as soon as they saw him. The three embraced, holding onto each other for a long time.

Trying to be strong, Stephen assured his sisters, "We'll get through this. I'll take care of you, always. We have each other, and we're lucky enough to have Uncle Peter and Aunt Sarah."

Confirming, Uncle Peter said, "Your FAMILY" We will never let you down.

Taking a moment to wipe his tears and compose himself, Uncle Peter said, "Your mum's fever persisted over the last few weeks. The doctors did everything they could. I'm so sorry.

"I made all the arrangements. We were just awaiting your return, Stephen."

"Why didn't you notify me sooner? Maybe I could have helped. Maybe I could have seen her one more time," Stephen cried.

"Your mother was so proud of you. She didn't want to alarm you, and she certainly didn't want to disrupt your studies. She asked us not to notify you. She believed, with all her heart, that she would recover, as did we all," Aunt Sarah explained. Bowing his head, Stephen accepted her explanation.

Parishioners gathered at the funeral with the family to pay their respects to Mrs. Jeanne Gano.

Stephen stood and spoke:

Thank you all for being here to grieve my mother's passing. My mother was beautiful on the inside and the outside. A great woman, she used to say, "Honor, education, and courage are the underpinnings of any fine person." She was the epitome of those words. She and dad taught my sisters and me to appreciate everything and to take nothing for granted. Her words shaped my life and her love, passion and enthusiasm were contagious to everyone she met.

Now that God has taken her away from us, I can only hope to make her and father proud.

Mama, Papa, may God bless you both.
We love you both. Amen

With heads bowed, a harmony of "Amen" followed.

The day after the funeral, Stephen repacked his belongings and prepared for the journey back to Rutgers. Hugging his Aunt and Uncle, he thanked them for all of their support, and especially for their generous care and provision for Morgan and Carly Ann.

"Don't worry about a thing, Stephen," Uncle Peter assured. "We'll be here for you and your sisters for all of our days. Focus on your studies. We'll see you during the semester break."

"Uncle Peter, I will do my very best. I can't thank you enough for all you do for my family and me. I will never forget," Stephen said humbly.

"We are FAMILY," Uncle Peter repeated.

Fighting tears, Morgan and Carly Ann hugged their brother tightly. Through their tears, they uttered, "We'll miss you!" and, "We love you!"

Hugging them equally as tight, Stephen told his sisters, "I love you both very much. Do all you can to help out your aunt and uncle.

Leaving the room, Uncle Peter announced, "I'll bring the carriage around."

Arriving at the train station exhausted, Stephen hugged his Uncle, thanking him again. In short order his train pulled in, and Stephen got on. He woke to the conductor's call, "NEW YORK CITY, ALL PASSENGERS EXIT, NEW YORK CITY."

Stephen changed trains and was soon on his way back to New Brunswick, New Jersey.

In the dark of night, Stephen made his way back to Hertzog Hall. Careful not to disturb anyone, he entered the building quietly. He found Claudius awake, reading by candlelight.

Somewhat startled by his arrival, Claudius greeted loudly, "Stephen, you're back!"

Waking to Claudius' voice, several men got up to offer Stephen their continued support. Stephen thanked them in kind.

Jacob asked, "How are your sisters holding up?"

"Thank the good lord for my aunt and uncle," Stephen answered. "The girls are distraught, of course, but they have good support."

"Welcome back Gano. We missed you around here," William said. Noting the hour, he encouraged, "Let's leave Gano to get some sleep. We'll see him in the morning."

"Thank you mates. I am so lucky to come back to you guys! I'll see you in the morning," Stephen said.

Fully exhausted, Stephen lay down in his bed and fell quickly to sleep.

CHAPTER 24

RISING EARLY, STEPHEN SAT AT THE TABLE STARING OUT THE window. Lost in thought, he watched the sun make a perfect entrance into the day. As the others awoke, they joined Stephen in the kitchen.

William happily informed Stephen, "A package arrived for you while you were in Boston. It's postmarked 'England'."

Perking up, Stephen took the package and shook it slightly, wondering what it contained. He heard a slight rattling sound. He assumed his girl-friend, Kathleen, heard about his mother's death and sent something to cheer him up. Eagerly, he opened the package and heard a gentle clanging sound as the contents fell to the floor.

Picking up the ring, he opened the accompanying letter and read:

To My Dear Stephen,

I write to you with shame and sorrow. In your absence, I have been unfaithful. I have found another man. Please accept the return of this promise ring. I hope you will find another woman more deserving than me.

You will always be my first love,
Kathleen

Furious, Stephen threw the ring against the wall as hard as he could. Ducking, his friends quickly retrieved it and handed it back to him. Wanting no part of the ring, he tossed it into the burning fireplace as his friends looked on in disbelief. He walked out of the room, slamming the door hard behind him.

Claudius picked up the letter that Stephen left on the table. He read it and informed the others, "It's what we expected would happen. The girl in England has moved onto other things."

Searching for Stephen, his friends finally found him sitting at the river's edge, staring straight ahead into the moonlight river. They surrounded him in silence.

The first to speak, Stephen said, "I thought it was a letter of condolence. I thought maybe she put some home baked cookies or something in the package. Instead she wrote to break her promise to me."

"At least she wrote," Claudius cajoled with a sly smile. Stephen tried to smile, releasing some of the stress they all felt.

"I'll be alright, mates," Stephen commented. I just have to sort this all out. It's a lot all at once, ya know? I should have brought Kathleen with me to the states. She's a sassy young lady and would have loved it here. What was I thinking?"

"You did nothing wrong, my friend," William supported. "It wasn't meant to be. God works in mysterious ways sometimes."

"William's right, Stephen. Besides, now you can pursue that "honey bell" in Princeton," Claudius agreed.

Stephen replied, "Claudius, you've been encouraging me to court Marianne from the minute I met you. She wants nothing to do with a foreigner like me."

"Not true," Claudius argued. Not true. I've been encouraging you to date her since I first set eyes on her, laughing out loud "Every time those Nassaus bully us, she comes to your aid."

"That's just her southern politeness," defended Stephen.

"Maybe so, but it's you she chooses to defend, not the rest of us poor, sorry fellows. We see the way she looks at you," Claudius pointed out.

Jacob added, "There's no mistaking her affection when she calls you."

Smiling, Stephen thanked his friends for their kindness and support, got up and began walking along the river. He turned back abruptly and shouted, "Mates, can I still get in on the Rumble?"

"You mean the football game?" William corrected. "Are you kidding? We'd love to have your help! You'll assure us our best chance to win. But why the sudden change of heart?"

Walking back to the group, Stephen explained, "Well mates, this seems like as good a time as any to tell you a few facts about my past." Taking a deep breath, he continued, "Like I told some of you my father was a legendary footballer in Rugby. But what I did not tell you was in the last game he and I played, he got tackled hard on the final play. He died as a result. It was terrible for my family and the entire town. The town elders banned the game in the form it was being played. My mother asked me to promise I'd never Rumble as long as she was on this good earth.

Now that she's left this good earth, there's nothing holding me back. I kept my promise. I haven't played since that awful day two years ago, and now she's left me to join my father. I'm going to honor my father, and my mother, by shutting those haughty, noses up, arrogant Nassaus once and for all. This I'll do for the Queensmen of today, and the Queensmen of tomorrow."

As Stephen spoke of the Nassaus, his face grew red and his voice grew loud. He focused all his grief on the Nassaus. Letting out his frustration and pain, he clenched his fists in the air and began chanting, "Shut the Nassaus up! Shut the Nassaus up!" The rest of the men joined in the chorus. Shut the Nassaus up ! Shut the Nassaus up! Shut the Nassaus up!

As the chanting subsided, William acknowledged, "This is great news, Stephen, really great news! Your past efforts and knowledge will help us be more confident and prepared."

The men embraced each other in a show of solid camaraderie. "Let's all be at the pre match bonfire the Thursday before the game". William told all the men.

CHAPTER 25

THE RUTGERS TEAM, MANY OF THEM IN ATTENDANCE WITH their friends and girlfriends, were gathered around a bonfire before the big game. Food and drink were abundant. There was an easy fellowship amongst the teammates.

As team captain, William welcomed the men and invited them to enjoy the evening. Looking around, he tried to encourage their confidence, telling them they looked prepared and ready. Noting Madison Ball's hair, he called, "Hey, Mad Dog, your hair looks a bit like a horse's tail!"

In response, Mad Dog admitted, "Ever since I was visited by Claudius and Stephen, I refused to cut it. It will offer some small measure of protection for the bashing my head is going to take. Hey, cap'n, we should use orange cloths to mark our mates in battle. Orange for the Duke of Orange."

Answering Mad Dog, Claudius said, "Yeah, I tried. I couldn't get orange. Besides, the Nassaus seem to like orange. I got scarlet colored scarves, we can turn into turbans instead."

"Well then, scarlet it is," William approved. He continued, "For those who haven't heard, Stephen Gano has agreed to help us win! Not just as an advisor, but as the brains and brawn we need to destroy the Nassaus."

The group of men and women shouted with delight.

As the crowd quieted, William requested, "In that we already have a full team of twenty five, I'll need someone to be first reserve if allowed, in order to give Stephen a spot as one of the two captains of the enemy goal, the other one being George Dixon."

Daniel immediately stood, looked at Stephen, and declared, "I will give you my spot, Gano. If we are to win, we need your expertise. I'm nothing but a body in this brawl. I want us to win. I'll be happy to help in any other way."

William accepted Daniel's offer, and complimented, "That is the spirit of a true team player!"

Stephen chimed in, "Yes, thank you for your selfless gesture, I won't disappoint you."

Carrying a mysterious burlap bag, Stephen took the opportunity to share what it contained. "In honor of my father and all footballers, I present the football that cost him his life," Stephen began. "But it doesn't symbolize his death; it symbolizes the game he loved and the game he won, over and over again. I've carried this ball with me from England as a reminder of my father's teachings and dedication."

Stephen passed the four panel pigskin ball into the crowd. They studied the names written onto the pigskin, and marveled at the difference between it and the rubber ball they would use in the game. "Remember fellas the hand signals I taught you, they came from him and will give us a great organizational advantage during our match".

As the evening concluded, William gave one more direction, "Remember Queensmen, the morning of the game we will be hosting our neighbors to the south. We will show them the best our town has to offer with courtesy and kindness. The Nassaus will be arriving on Saturday at ten o'clock. We will show them every consideration... at least until the game begins. "

In various stages of inebriation, the men and women laughed at William's last remark. Stretching and yawning, most dispersed. Very drunk, Claudius, Mad Dog, and Henry Steele stayed behind with Howard Fuller. After working on a new cheer song, Claudius had an idea. Feeling feisty, he suggested, "Let's go to The College of New Jersey and give the big cannon a fresh coat of red paint."

Henry Steele, maintaining some rational thought, responded, "Not tonight. We don't want to give the Nassaus any extra motivational anger with which to play the game."

"Good point," Mad Dog agreed. "Let's leave that fun for the spring."

CHAPTER 26

PRINCETON. GETTING AN EARLY START FOR THE GAME, STU-
dents and friends were waiting for the Dinky at the station alongside William
Gummere and most of his team. It was Saturday morning, seven o'clock
when the three-car, rickety, black-paneled, steam engine pulled into the
campus station. Pushing their way on, bundled for the November weather,
approximately fifty tailgaters out of a town of 2500 were carrying the day's
necessities: baskets of food, towels, cigars, blankets, and more. Two boys snuck
a wooden keg on board, and two others were playing Confederate Army Civil
War battle calls on their drums as they entered the train car.

The Dinky was nearly full before the whole team boarded. Eager to
make the short ride, they would all switch to the main line train that would
deliver them to New Brunswick. As Bill Gummere approached, the conductor asked, "How many more need to board?"

Gummere responded, "A few more, sir. I see them coming now. We're
headed to Rutgers to show those Queensmen who're superior once again,
this time on the football field."

"I heard about the game," the conductor said. "We're going to be more
than full. Take a seat if you can find one. Otherwise, find something to hold
onto."

Aboard the train, the excitement was escalating. People were loud and
giddy, anticipating what was to come. The drummers continued.

Taking Marianne's hand, "Tar Heel" helped his sister up the steps
and onto the train car. He followed her on, trailed by a few dawdling team
members. Once the men were all on board, the conductor inquired, "I heard
the Queensmen made the challenge?"

"They did, fools that they are," "Tar Heel" answered. "Now we'll just have to slam them again, if this old steamer can get us to the next train. Maybe after this slaughter, they'll accept that we are the better school, with the better men, once and for all."

"Oh, don't you worry about this old steamer," the conductor assured, "it'll make it, no problem. You just make the Nassaus proud."

With great billowing black smoke belching from the smokestack, the overloaded Dinky began to move slowly out of the station, straining from the weight. As the drums beat civil war battle calls and marching songs, some riders were singing "Old Nassau." With plenty of laughter and great commotion, the men of Nassau were on their way to the Rumble.

By ten o'clock, the good people of New Brunswick were also making their way to the field before the game carrying baskets of food and beverages, setting up their tailgates at the end of the horse drawn wagons, they then went on to claim the best viewing spots. The Queensmen could hear the boisterous Nassaus coming into the station as they waved their arms and stuck their heads out of the windows of the train, shouting and singing. More than sixty passengers exited the train. Many had already begun imbibing. As the train came to a halt, the raucous crowd burst into the station with great fanfare.

Waiting for their nemeses, Claudius warned, "Here they come."

As the team got off the train, William Gummere looked for William Leggett. In short order, the two connected. As Gummere walked toward Leggett, they both extended their hands for a hardy handshake.

Leggett was the first to speak, "Good morning Captain Gummere," he said. "Welcome to New Brunswick. We'd like to give you a tour of our humble town and have you join us for a meal before the game."

"You are true gentlemen of sport, thank you," Gummere replied.

"We will be, right up until the first buck," Leggett responded. "Then we will take off the white gloves and put on the brass knuckles."

Staring into each other's eyes, Leggett and Gummere smiled, fully aware of the truth of that statement. They shook hands again.

The men of both teams greeted each other with proper handshakes and jovial attitudes. The Rutgers men walked with the Nassaus and the women who accompanied them, graciously showing them what the town had to offer. The Queensmen were keenly aware of the many beautiful women accompanying the Nassaus. Stephen was especially aware of Marianne.

Arriving at the pool hall, several men chose to shoot a few assorted billiard games rather than continue the tour. Passing Northrop's, William Leggett announced, "And this is the famous Northrop's Tavern. God willing, after the game, we'll join here for food, drinks and more good times."

As they approached the Raritan River, a steamship was making its way toward New York City. Small fishing boats spotted the water's landscape. One of the Princeton men mentioned the beauty of the evergreens that lined the banks.

Leggett explained, "The river ties into the canals that run through your fair city, as well as ours, and ultimately connects the Atlantic Ocean to the Delaware River. Shipments of goods run up and down this river, day in and day out, destined for Philadelphia or New York. From those ports, goods can go anywhere in the world.

William Gummere chuckled as he whispered to a buddy, "I wonder how the mysterious missing cannon was stolen."

While the men stood looking at the water, a host of women arrived with blankets, baskets of food, and plenty to drink. Lunch was ready. The men sent runners to retrieve those who lingered at the pool hall.

The teams and their guests made themselves comfortable and ate on the banks. Taking care of business, William Leggett approached William Gummere and asked, "Do we have any final knotty points to sort out?"

"Just fair catch and free kick. We'd still like to have them as a rule of play," Gummere requested.

Leggett, wanting to accommodate, began, "Well, in the spirit of..."

Listening to the exchange, Stephen cut off his captain saying, "We'll have none of that. An agreement is an agreement, and we agreed not to have the fair catch, free kick. The rules stand as previously discussed."

Rethinking his overly generous and self-sabotaging initial response, Leggett agreed with Stephen.

"Alright," Gummere agreed, "but in the next game, home team rules will apply."

In agreement, Leggett asked, "Anything else we need to discuss?"

"Can't think of anything," Gummere responded, shaking his head left to right.

"Great, eat up. We'll all need our strength. We'll have a short time to rest before the first mount," Leggett informed.

Having had their fill of food and drink, the teams parted ways. They would spend the remaining time before the game resting and working through last minute strategies.

CHAPTER 27

FED AND RESTED, AT 2:30 P.M. WILLIAM LEGGETT PROMPTED his team to move toward Sicard Street. William Gummere did the same. As they neared Commons Field, the men could hear the murmur of those assembled, waiting for the game to begin. Drums beats roared, filling the spectator's ears.

Back at Olde Queens, biblical literature professor Theodore Sanford; William Campbell, the school's president; George Cook, head of the scientific school and Reverend Chester David Hartranft were debating the merits of the upcoming game. The crackling fire was virtually silenced by the booming voices.

"Are you aware, Reverend, that the men of Nassau have been here all morning?" the professor began. "And for a football game no less!"

Reverend Hartranft politely replied, "Yes, I am aware, good sir. The Queensmen are scheduled to beat those Nassau's at the Sicard Street field today. The game will be starting within the hour."

"You seem to know all the details, Reverend!" the professor accused. "How did this devilish game come to be, and what is your involvement?"

"Yes, I'd like to know as well," President Campbell chimed in.

Professor Cook picked up a copy of the New York Evening Post, reading and I Quote "Football so brutal it makes the same impression as a bull fight"

"I must confess," stated the Reverend, "I have helped our boys to arrange this match and two more if necessary. It's time to finally win our honor back from those Nassau's, and this is the way to do it!"

Enraged, the professor shouted, "You've been helping? What honor is to be gained from such a vile, prehistoric, brutal game?"

Trying to remain calm, the Reverend explained, "Since they stole our cannon, the Nassaus' chronic boasting has taken a toll on us. The 'diamond disaster' this past spring accelerated their abuse. They are constantly harassing our boys and puffing out their chests like peacocks. They are not superior, and we need to show them such!"

"Superiority is not decided on a diamond, a field, or by cannon theft!" Professor Sanford shouted, his face turning red. "It's decided in the class-room. Brainpower can show those braggards who are the superior men, not playing a brutal, violent game. 'Legal murdering' is how some have framed it. I DEMAND YOU CALL OFF THIS BRAWL RIGHT NOW!"

With his temper and blood pressure growing, professor Sanford addressed President Campbell, insisting, "Call your cronies in Princeton and have them call back their boys. This is not going to happen on my watch!"

"I beg to differ with you, Theodore," the Reverend said, trying to diffuse the extreme hostility being projected, "The lessons learned by such a match rival the best of any classroom lessons. The men learn courage, discipline, hard work, teamwork, and persistence. In a selfish world, football is the most unselfish of endeavors. The whole team learns to win or lose together."

"There's too much risk for anything worthwhile to be learned," Professor Sanford countered, calming slightly. "Plus, it distracts the entire student body from their required studies. I've been wondering why the men have seemed so disconnected lately. I thought it might be the impending holidays."

"This match does seem to be distracting the men from their studies," President Campbell asserted. "I'm not at all happy with this illegal activity."

"While you have some good points," Reverend Hartranft countered, "the love of physical competition should be in every boy's heritage. This love can guide them through wholesome channels of growth, enhancing their educational experience. It unifies and bonds the diverse, growing student body, teaching them the importance of trust, teamwork, camaraderie, and commitment. The Reverend continued.

"Professor Sanford, with any luck, this will be the closest any of these men come to the physical and psychological demands of war. Football requires strategy, courage, and determination. These are the characteristics we want our boys to learn here at Rutgers and take these skills to the great growing country in which we live."

"You have it all wrong, good Reverend," the professor disputed. "We can teach them those things in the classroom. There is no good reason for them to risk their lives playing games. Football has no place at any respectable college."

Reverend Hartranft had had enough; he was no longer calm. "This is a great opportunity for our men," the Reverend hollered. "There is no classroom here, or anywhere, that offers our men a better chance to grow and evolve. And they are not required to play this game, they have chosen to! The game is on and nothing you say will stop it!"

Disgusted, crotchety Professor Sanford walked out of the room, slamming the office door behind him. Leaving Olde Queens Hall, he slammed the great wooden entrance door as well. He got on a rickety, black bicycle and pedaled away, shouting and flailing his hands in the air. President Campbell shook his head in disapproval of the whole affair. The Reverend left the room and headed to the field to support his team.

Chapter 28

At the field, Princeton fans were chanting, "Sis boom ba, Princeton, Princeton, OOOOORAAAA, OOOORAAAA." With Civil War battle calls beating steadily in the background.

Sawdust marked the boundaries for the day's game and a large American Flag flapped in the wind, welcoming the many spectators who were settling into finding the best vantage points for sitting or standing around the field, perching on fences, on horse drawn buckboard wagons and open grassy areas. Scents of meat grilling, cigars smoking, and beer spilling were carried by the breeze as tailgaters feasted.

Grimly, the Rutgers team members stripped off their overcoats, vests, and hats, and threw them toward the excited crowd. They turned their suspenders to belts, red scarves into turbans and rolled up their trousers and shirt sleeves.

One of the older members of the team, a big, energetic fellow, D.D. Williamson ran, wiggled and waved to his teammates and the spectators, showing off his long red shirt and scarlet turban. In a show of solidarity, many of the Rutgers fans took off their red scarves and wrapped them around their heads like turbans mirroring the team in support.

Laughing, Claudius shouted, "D. D., we said to wear a scarlet turban! Not a red cape the color of Ganos head!"

Amused and a little envious, "Tar Heel" shouted across the field, "Nice that you marked your boys so well for slaughter."

As Stephen had seen so many times in his past, the team captains walked to center field and heartily shook hands. The men on either side were readily sizing up their competition. Looking to the sideline, Stephen spotted Marianne standing by the fence, waving politely.

"Captain Gummere," Leggett said, extending his hand. "Welcome to Commons Field."

Shaking his hand, Gummere replied, "Good day for a football game! Feels like snow. Have you chosen a referee?"

"Yes, it will be Alexander Johnston," Leggett responded.

"Good. Ours will be James Chambers," Gummere announced, nodding for Alexander to join them.

"Agreed," Legget replied, motioning his referee to join them as well.

As Chambers ran over holding the ball, Gummere caught sight of it. "Is that the game ball?" he asked, surprised.

Gummere held out his hand, silently directing the referee to give it to him. The referee obliged, putting the thick, small, black rubber ball in his hands. "This seems quite small," Gummere commented." Squeezing the ball.

Leggett responded, "Bounce it, you'll see it's quite lively."

After bouncing the small ball several times, Gummere nodded his approval. He handed it back to the referee.

"Are we ready for the coin toss?" With a nod, both captains indicated they were ready.

Retrieving a silver dollar from his pocket, the referee said, "Nassaus made the first call. Winner will choose their defensive goal."

The referee threw the coin up in the air and Captain Gummere called, "Heads." "Tails it is! The choice goes to the Queensman," stated the referee.

Leggett pointed into the breeze toward the uprights.

Once again the referee threw the coin into the air. Captain Legget called, "Heads."

"Tails it is," shouted the referee. "Nassaus', you get the first buck."

The captains shook hands and returned to their teams.

"They get first buck," Leggett told his squad. "We chose defense of the goal; we're going with the wind to start."

Freshman made up nearly half their team. Nonetheless, the Queensmen felt confident and ready. They looked over the men of Princeton and discussed who they thought was vulnerable as well as who they thought would present their strongest challenge. There were no freshmen on the Princeton team.

"ARE WE READY?" Captain Legget shouted. "Assigned and ready," came Stephen's reply.

Grunting and hollering, the Queensmen gathered their team spirit. Meanwhile, on the other side, William Gummere shouted, "Are the Nassaus ready?"

A unified team barked back, "Ready captain," was returned.

Using his boot heel, Gummere dug a tee in the hard dirt and placed the ball for first buck. The two teams took almost identical places on the field. Each team placed two captains at their enemy goal, six fielders on each side, and eleven bulldozers or bulldogs in the center.

The Nassuas were using the Apache war scream trying to intimidate the Queensmen and the crowd, yelling ay-ayay-ayay-ya-yaya- with all looking on as the game was about to begin.

On the sideline, Marianne leaned toward another woman and asked, "Did you see that Stephen Gano is playing today?"

"You mean that cute, well-mannered, well-everything, Englishman?" the woman said, her cheeks blushing red.

Also blushing, Marianne agreed, "Yes, and there he is!" she said pointing.

The woman whispered, "Did you hear about that poor man's recent hardship? His father died playing this very game, and his mother just died suddenly two weeks ago."

Another woman leaning forward whispered, "And I heard his English girlfriend sent him back her promise ring."

Choking up, Marianne watched Stephen's every move. Him signaling with hands the next intended play when the ball comes their way.

Badly executed, Gummere's kick went far off to the right toward the Queensmen goal. The Queensmen immediately trounced the ball and formed a punishing wedge. The interlocked men running crushed everyone that got in their way. Arriving at the goal, Stephen got the ball from a teammate and kicked the ball hard and it sailed between the goal posts. Raising his arms upright, the referee signaled the score.

Rutgers, 1: The College of New Jersey, 0

The crowd was on their feet, cheering and hollering in a boisterous frenzy. Marianne was no different. Though she was from Princeton, the sister of a Nassau, seeing Rutgers and Stephen score the first goal made her proud. As a Rutgers man walked by with extra scarlet scarves, Marianne took one and tied it around her braided bun. Excitement was in the air.

Conferencing with Big Mike, William Gummere insisted, "Mike, we need you to break that massing (wedge) play."

"I will cap'n," Big Mike agreed with terror in his eyes. "I'll break 'em apart like I was breaking twigs."

Since the scoring team got the buck, Rutgers had the ball. The Rutgers bulldozers pounded on the buck. They passed it to their best dribbler and once again five men with locked arms, destroyed anyone who tried to interfere. Gaining momentum, the Rutgers men felt overly confident. Big Mike then brutally crashed into the flying wedge, scattering the men like sticks as he had promised. Stunned, the Rutgers men lost the ball. Finding it at their feet, the Nassaus took control. Big Mike took the long shot, kicking the ball hard. It flew through the goalposts, tying the game.

Rutgers, 1: The College of New Jersey, 1

Fully charged, William Gummere shouted, "Great play Big Mike. Keep it coming!"

Bloodied, Big Mike shook his head in agreement. He readied the ball on a boot made tee. Nassau kicked, trapped the ball, and formed a wedge of their own. George Large, determined and angry, easily broke the Nassau wedge.

Back and forth the ball went, from one team to the other. Men were taking a beating and kept up the fight. As goal attempts were being blocked or missed at both sides, Mad Dog Madison revved up his game. Running past the ball, he kicked it backwards with his heel, landing it by the Princeton goal. Easily, Dixon of Rutgers retrieved the ball and kicked it through the posts.

Rutgers, 2: The College of New Jersey, 1

As the men switched sides after each score, Claudius called to Dixon, "Great play!"

Dixon, tired and bloody, acknowledged the compliment with a nod. As others shouted accolades to Dixon, it was clear the Queensmen camaraderie was strong.

The Queensman kicked the ball again towards the Princeton goal. Running down the field, the Rutgers wedge once again faced the brutal determination of Big Mike. With the Rutgers wedge scattered, William Gummere got control of the ball and dribbled it to the Rutgers goal posts. Kicking it through the posts, the referee signaled a score.

Rutgers, 2: The College of New Jersey, 2

Riding up on his bicycle next to the field where everyone could see him, Professor Sanford yelled at the players, "You will come to no good Christian end. Shame on you all!"

On the field, "Tar Heel" shouted, "Come on Nassaus, we have to take the lead on these men. Don't let 'em score again!"

Mustering their energy, the Nassaus shook their heads in fervent agreement.

With the next buck, Stephen got the ball and single handedly dribbled it down the field with his feet to kick through another goal.

Rutgers, 3: The College of New Jersey, 2

Forgetting that the rules excluded fair catch, a Princeton man motioned for the play. Besides the man being brutally clobbered, the referee threw a penalty flag in the air. With The College of New Jersey losing any semblance of organization, the Rutgers team quickly got the penalty kick into their possession. With Stephen leading the way, they pushed through the melee to score again. The Queensmen were now unified for one outcome: Victory.

Rutgers, 4: The College of New Jersey, 2

"Bring it together, dozers!" William Gummere screamed to his men. He was definitely becoming worried.

The team huddled to discuss strategy. Tired and bloody, they were already unhinged. Their captain did his best to encourage and unite them.

"Keep the ball high," Captain Gummere commanded. "If we don't want to go home defeated, we have to score four more! Smash these Queensmen! We can play better than this!"

The men knew the stakes. They would never live down a defeat to Rutgers.

"And for heaven's sake, keep that ball away from the red-haired Englishman! He's killing us out there! He's a kicking machine on the field!" Gummere added.

With no real breaks in play, the men were emotionally taxed. Bloody noses, cuts, and ghastly bruises dominated the view. The players were exhausted. They sighed in relief when the ball went out of bounds, for the occasional foul called or for a pause to inflate the ball.

Once again, the buck went to Rutgers. There was a race to retrieve the rolling ball. As Big Mike and George Large neared the fence in pursuit of the round rubber sphere, the crowd went wild. Big Mike running fast crushed George Large, pushing him face first into the fence knocking him out cold. Perched onlookers were also knocked down off the fence screaming, including Marianne. A bucket of icy cold water was quickly taken from a nearby horse trough and was thrown onto George's head. Sputtering awake, he staggered to his feet and gladly went back into the fray.

Seeing her fall, Stephen rushed to Marianne's side. Helping her up, he questioned whether she was hurt. Assuring him she was fine, Marianne encouraged Stephen to return to the field.

Undeterred by the melee, Jacob took control of the ball and began moving it toward his own goal by mistake. Confused and disoriented by the commotion in the crowd, Jacob's attempt on the goal was blocked by his own team.

"Jacob," Leggett screamed, "you're going the wrong way!"

A Princeton man seized the golden opportunity, kicking and taking the ball away from Jacob and through the uprights to score one for the Nassau's.

Rutgers, 4: The College of New Jersey, 3

"Let's keep on 'em," Big Mike yelled, "Three more goals Nassaus! Just three more!" again more of the Apache screams trying to excite his mates. AYA, AYAYA, AYA.

Sheepishly, Jacob apologized, "Sorry fellas, I got all twisted up."

The Nassaus had the buck. Mauling, kicking, moving the ball toward the enemy goal led by Big Mike, the Princeton men made short work of pushing the ball through the uprights for another quick score. The men on the field were visibly exhausted, with many limping and bleeding.

Rutgers, 4: The College of New Jersey, 4

With the score tied, Big Mike yelled, "Let's keep on 'em! Two more goals!"

Invoking the Apache battle cry once again, the Nassaus and spectators responded "AYA AYA YA YAY AYAY!"

With that, Big Mike mounted and bucked the ball. The crowd was frenetic: screaming and shouting advice for how their team should proceed to insure a win. Princeton supporters invoked and repeated the "rocket call, "Sizz boom bah, sizz boom bah, hooray, hooray, hooray, tiger, tiger, tiger, Princeton, Princeton, Princeton." The Civil War drum beats played faster and faster as the crowd got louder and louder in support of what they were watching.

"Crush 'em," shouted a Rutgers spectator. "Smash 'em again! You can do it!"

Noticing a man to his left, writing, the spectator questioned, "What are you writing?"

"I'm here for the new school newspaper, the Daily Targum," the man replied. The Rutgers team's captain is the editor, he told me to cover this spectacle. "I'm trying to capture the excitement of the game. It's hard to put into words."

"Targum, that was code for cheat sheets when I was in school a few years back," the spectator commented.

"Yes, that's right," the journalist agreed. "Hopefully that'll help you to remember the name and make you want to read it."

The spectator assured me, "I'll definitely pick one up if I see it!"

Hearing William Leggett shouting, their attention was succinctly brought back to the game.

"Keep that ball on the ground," Leggett demanded. "Don't let them use their height advantage." Hand signals calling out the next attack.

Big Mike bucked the ball again. Rutgers' players took control and formed another flying wedge and Big Mike broke it up again in seconds. Back and forth, the violence continued. Keeping the ball low was working to the Queensmen advantage.

"Get the ball to our captains at the enemy goal," Stephen yelled angrily. "We have to take the egg and win this thing!"

Finally, using their speed and agility, the Queensmen got the ball to Stephen as planned. He kicked it through the goalposts for another score.

Rutgers, 5: The College of New Jersey, 4

William Leggett shouted to Stephen, "Great kick Gano! One more to win back our honor! JUST ONE MORE!!"

"Come on mates, let's put 'em out of their misery!" Stephen shouted, "Get that ball to me! I promise I'll shut those Nassaus up for good!"

Frantic with excitement, the Rutgers crowd was up on their feet, screaming with excitement, and then chanting "RUTGERS! RUTGERS! RUTGERS! RUTGERS! As the chant grew louder and faster, so, too, did the drumbeats.

The Queensmen had the buck and George Large got the ball. Immediately he passed it to Stephen, who dribbled it down the field expertly. As he set up the kick, two defenders ran to block his attempt. Getting the kickoff, the defenders collided with Stephen, bringing them all to the ground. The ball flew through the uprights.

Rutgers, 6: The College of New Jersey, 4

Rutgers had won the match! As the Queensmen surrounded Stephen to celebrate, they realized he and the defenders were not moving.

"Get up!" men were shouting.

The defenders began to move, and a partial sigh of relief rippled through the crowd. Stephen Gano was still motionless.

With all eyes on Stephen, no one had dared breathe. As he slowly got up, the celebration was swift! Marriane came running over and gave Stephen a big hug and congratulated him on his fine play.

The tired teams respectfully embraced and shook hands in a polite round of congratulations. Spectators poured forth onto the field, screaming and singing the praises of both sides. Congratulations poured forth for the Queensmen.

Still Groggy and confused, Stephen asked, "Did the ball I kicked make it through the posts?"

"You bet it did, Stephen," William Leggett responded. "You're our hero! You scored the winning goal!"

William Gummere slowly approached William Leggett to congratulate him. "Great game Leggett! Your boys gave it to us solid today. And who is that red haired Scottish terror?"

Standing close to Stephen, Leggett grabbed Stephen by the shoulder and introduced, "This man here is Stephen Gano. He came from across the pond to help us out."

Shaking his head, Gummere praised, "You were simply marvelous."

Changing the subject, Captain Leggett walking slowly asked, "After we all get cleaned up we'll see you all at Northrop's Tavern for supper then?"

"It'll be a welcome consolation for us, thank you," Captain Gummere replied. "There will be a bounty of game birds, food and kegs at our disposal," Leggett informed.

Overhearing the invitation, a bloodied Big Mike commented, "We'll dispose of them alright! Congratulating the Rutgers team, all the members of both squads embraced after this epic battle of will.

With that, both teams headed back to town to clean up. As they walked, they reviewed the day's battle. Marianne left Stephen's side to join her brother and offer her support.

"That polite gentleman you met on the train gave us quite a thrashing, didn't he?" "Tar Heel" commented to his sister.

"That he did, "Tar Heel"," Marianne said dreamily.

CHAPTER 29

THAT NIGHT, ABOUT TWO HUNDRED PEOPLE ASSEMBLED IN
and around Northrop's Tavern. A small bonfire glowed in the courtyard
behind the tavern. It was a festive college scene with both sides sharing game
highlights, cheers, chants, and songs, showing school pride. Storytelling
was fanciful, with beer and pipe sessions in full swing the fun was starting
to begin.

William Gummere walked to the center of the crowd, and with a
booming voice, commanded the attention of all. Holding the game ball high
over his head, he began, "Before we dig in to this great bounty, I would like to
bestow this game ball upon the mighty Queensmen. They proved themselves
superior to us Nassaus today. They have also proven themselves to be gracious
hosts and gentlemen, and we are grateful for their generosity." Turning to
Captain William Leggett, he continued, "You and your team were consis-
tently in the right place at the right time. You knew when to kick and when
to push. I hereby bestow this winning game ball upon you and your mates."

Cheers, hoots, and hollers erupted from the crowd.

William Leggett took the ball and the spotlight, saying, "I accept this
ball from our neighbors to the south. They have also been true gentlemen
of sport and competition. This ball belongs to a gentleman and friend who
I will always remember for his courage, honor and integrity. He was a force
to be reckoned with today, but more than that, without his expertise and
determination, as well as his precision and talent, we would likely be offering
this ball to the Nassaus. I think everyone will agree, Stephen Gano deserves
this ball more than anyone else other than maybe George Large and his great

battles with the 'Giant' they call Mike.`` The crowd looking at them both admiringly, erupts in great laughter and excited celebration.

With that, William Leggett handed the ball to Stephen. The room filled with the sound of applause, hoots and hollers.

Timidly and with great humility, Stephen shook his captain's hand. He accepted the ball without fanfare or statement then held it up high for all to see. As Captain Leggett invited everyone to begin the feast, many rushed to Stephen, offering congratulations.

"Tar Heel" was the first to speak to Stephen, "You were truly brilliant out there. I apologize for all my past rudeness."

Stephen replied, "Without your rudeness, I might not have been half as inspired to beat you today!" Smiling.

While "Tar Heel" and Stephen talked, Marianne made her way over to join them. "Congratulations again, Stephen," Marianne said shyly.

"Thank you! How long was I out?" Stephen asked.

"Too long," Marianne replied. "You had me half frightened to death!"

"You frightened me as well. I'm so sorry you got knocked off the fence while you were watching the game. Are you okay?" Stephen questioned with concern.

"Yes. It was pretty exciting, actually. Nothing like what you boys went through on that field!" Marianne commented. "I'm fine, just a scratch or two."

With "Tar Heel" listening to every word, Stephen asked, "Would you like to take a walk with me? We could go to the river and watch the moonrise."

Marianne glanced at her brother, seeking approval. With a nod, "Tar Heel" gave his consent.

Walking away from the tavern, handing the game ball to Marianne to look at, it was some time before the sounds of celebration quieted. Once they did, Marianne said, "I'm sorry for being so selfish, Stephen."

"Selfish?" Stephen replied, surprised by the comment.

"Back on the train," Marianne explained, "I rambled on about me and mine, but didn't let you speak long enough to hear about you, your family and your father. I talked too much!"

"I enjoyed hearing every word you spoke, Marianne!" Stephen admitted. "Your voice was music to my ears, and I loved hearing every detail."

"Stephen, I don't mean to be rude, but has your girlfriend ever come to visit you here in the states?" Marianne questioned.

Surprised, Stephen asked, "How did you know about Kathleen?"

"I overheard some of the girls gossiping while we were watching the game," Marianne said.

"Wow, I didn't realize people were talking about me," Stephen remarked. "I don't have a girlfriend anymore. She found someone else back home in England."

"I'm sorry, Stephen," Marianne consoled.

"Don't be, Marianne. I think it's for the best," Stephen replied. "So which of those men who are always surrounding you is courting you?"

"Courting me?" Marianne said with a mile-wide smile, "Those men annoy me! They're my brother's friends. They think they have to protect me. That or they all want to date me according to my mother. But according to my brother, they think I'm an 'ice queen.' "Tar Heel" says they think I'm beautiful on the outside and cold on the inside. I promised I'd be a little more friendly, but I have no interest in any of them!"

"Hmmm, ice queen, that's not something I'd ever call you," Stephen responded. "I find you to be warm and friendly, and engaging. I'd like to see you more, Marianne. I'd like to melt any remaining ice and really get to know you. Would that be alright?"

"Are you asking me to go steady with you?" Marianne clarified.

"I would like that very much," Stephen answered. Gently reaching for Marianne's hand, the two strolled along the river seeing where it connected to the canal.

Suddenly struck with a thought, Stephen exclaimed, "So that's how they stole it!" "Stole what?" Marianne asked, confused.

"The big cannon!" Stephen said as though he just discovered the key to life. "I think the Nassaus used the canal to transport the big cannon, not the roads!"

Marianne and Stephen talked into the night. Realizing it had gotten very late, they headed toward the train station. "Tar Heel" and his friends were waiting nervously for Marianne's return. Fortunately, they arrived just in time for Marianne to board the owl back to Princeton.

As the train left the station, Marianne smiled and waved to Stephen, subtly throwing him a kiss through the open window. The men of Nassau, beaten, vowed to get even in the next week's rematch. Having accompanied the Nassaus to the train station, Stephen's friends were eager to hear all about his sudden disappearance from the tavern.

"I think you'll be seeing a lot more of Miss Marianne Glen, gentlemen," Stephen stated, deliberately vague on details.

"Hopefully she'll bring her friends!" Claudius interjected.

Tired, but fueled by their win, the boys talked about the gameday as they walked back to Hertzog Hall. Feeling the camaraderie, they began to sing the new Rutgers song their friend Howard Newton Fuller had been writing: "On the Banks of the Old Raritan." Passing Old Queens, Claudius had an idea. Motioning the others to join him, they ran up the stairs and made their way to the bell cupola. With great jubilance, they rang the bell in celebration of their victory for all to hear. Once again, they were the honorable men of Rutgers!

EPILOGUE

A WEEK LATER THE SECOND GAME OF THE "BEST OF THREE" was played on the College of New Jersey campus. The Nassau's evoked the rule of fair catch and free kick and won with a score of eight to zero.

United, the faculty of both schools barred the students from playing the third and final game. They determined that the disruption to both student bodies was too great. Nonetheless the men of Rutgers, the Queensmen had earned the abiding respect from the men of The College of New Jersey, the Nassaus. Thus, linking the schools' distinguished legacies forever together.

Shortly thereafter football games were officially sanctioned by the Colonial Colleges in the United States and Universities in Europe, Canada and Australia. From that time forward Football, Soccer and Rugby went their separate ways. Formalizing all the backyard rules that were being played the previous centuries was the next task of all the schools to allow for consistent play amongst them all, and the rules of all have been evolving ever since.

The Daily Fredonian New Brunswick's newspaper
November, 1869 account of the first game signed, "Spectator"

'HURRAH FOR THE BOYS OF GOOD OLD RUTGERS,' WHO ARE
waking up as was fully demonstrated last Saturday afternoon, in the lively,
but tough game of football.

"Our neighbor, Princeton, sent her chosen twenty-four stalwart men,
and one Goliath to combat our twenty-five striplings. There is not recorded
in the history of the Olympic games a more interesting and decisive match,
played in so short a time, by such a number of contestants as this game was.
Rutgers led off by winning the first inning amid the vociferous cheering
of the bystanders. Princeton seemed to play a little wild at the beginning,
but the second inning they recovered themselves, and came out victors. So
it continued, off and on, one gaining, then the other, until the ninth and
tenth inning, when, notwithstanding the desperate efforts of the Princeton
giants, Rutgers quickly and boldly followed in successive victory, giving
them six runs to four of Princeton. Thereby coming off conquerors, which
was hailed with exulting shouts of applause by the admirers of Rutgers. The
victorious twenty-five then gave three rousing cheers and a 'tiger' which was
followed by the Princeton twenty-five cheering, and a something sounding
very much like 'Ou ! Bum ! Haugh ! The game just ended in good feeling,
although during the playing we observed some rather unnecessary sparring
on the part of a few of the Princeton 'Philistines.' 'All is well that ends well.'
Through the generous liberality of the students of Rutgers College, a bountiful entertainment was prepared for our Princeton friends, at the favorite
resort in Church Street known as Northrop's, where "mine host" and his
estimable lady know how to get up a good supper. May they live long to serve
the students of Rutgers thus. How are you seventy- three? So ends a pleasant
rivalry between sister Colleges, of which there are none more honorable in
the land. Princeton did well, but Rutgers did better, and let it continue to
be, not alone on athletic sports, but also in the more energetic of the mind.

The Targum, the Rutgers Newspaper
November 6th, 1869 account of the First game.
THE FOOT-BALL MATCH.

ON SATURDAY, NOVEMBER 6TH, PRINCETON SENT TWEN-ty-five picked men to play our twenty-five a match game of foot-ball. the strangers came up in the 10 o'clock train, and brought a good number of backers with them. After dinner, and a stroll around the town, during which stroll billiards received a good deal of attention, the crowds began to assemble at the ball ground, which, for the benefit of the ignorant, we would say,is a lot about a hundred yards wide, extending from College ave to Sicard-street. Previous to calling the game,the ground presented an animated picture. Grim-looking players were silently stripping each one surrounded by sym-pathising friends, while around each of the captains was a little crowd, in tent upon giving advice, and saying as much as possible. The appearance of the Princeton men was very different from that of our own players. They were almost without exception tall and muscular, while the majority of our twenty-five are small and light, but possess the merit of being up to much more than they look.

Very few were the preliminaries, and they were quickly agreed upon. The Princeton captain for some reason or other, gave up every point to our men without contesting one. The only material points were, that Princeton gave up "free kicks," were by a player, when he catches the ball in the air is allowed to kick it without hindrance. On the other hand, our practice of "babying" the ball on the start was discarded, and the ball was mounted,in every instance, by a vigorous "long kick."

Princeton won the toss, and chose the first mount, rather oddly, since it had been agreed to the ball against the wind. At 3 P.M. the game was called. The Princetonians suffered from making a very bad "mount," or "buck" as they call it; the effects of which were not remedies before the sides closed, and after a brief struggle, Rutgers drove it home, and won amid great applause from the crowd. The sides were changed, Rutgers started the ball, and after a somewhat longer fight, Princeton made it a tie by a well directed kick, from a gentleman whose name we do not know, but did the best kicking for the Princeton side.

To describe the varying fortunes of the match, game by game, would be a waste of labor, for every game was like the one before. There was the same head, long running wild shouting and frantic kicking. In every game the cool goaltenders saved the Rutgers goal half a dozen times; in every game the heavy charger of the Princeton side overthrew everything he came in contact with; and in every game, just when the interest in one of those delightful rushes at the fence was culminating, the persecuted ball would fly for refuge into the next lot, and produce a cessation of hostilities until, after the invariable "foul," it was put in straight.

Well, at least we won the match, having won the 1st,3d,5th,6th,9th,and 10th games; leaving Princeton the 2d.4th,7th,8th. The seventh game would probably have been added to our score but for one of our players, who, in his ardor, forgot which way he was kicking, a mistake which he fully atoned for afterward. To sum up. Princeton had the most muscle, but didn't kick very well, and wanted organization. They evidently don't like to kick the ball on the ground. Our men, on the other hand, though comparatively weak, ran well and kicked well throughout. But their great point was their organization, for which great praise is due to the captain, Leggett, '72'. The right men were always in the right place.

After the match, the players had an amicable "feed" together and at 8 o'clock our guests went home, in high good spirits, but thirsting to beat us next time, if they can.

The Targum account as it appeared,
of the second game played in Princeton
the following Saturday, November 13th, 1869.
PRINCETON vs. RUTGERS.

THE SECOND OF THREE GAMES OF FOOT BALL BETWEEN
Princeton and Rutgers was won by the former at their ball-grounds, on
Saturday, the 13th inst. Eight out of fifteen was the game, but as Princeton
won the first eight the innings were not played. The style of playing differs,
materially, in the two Colleges. A fly, or first bound catch, entitles to a "free
kick," a la Princeton. We bat with hands, feet, head, sideways, backwards,
any way to get the ball along. We must say that we think our style much
more exciting, and more as Foot-Ball should be. After the regular game
two innings were played after our fashion, and we won them. It is but fair to
our twenty-five to say that they never have practiced the "free-kick" system.
At half-past six we sat down to a very fine supper, prepared for us by our
hosts. Speeches and songs accompanied, of course, by the study of practi-
cal gastronomy, passed the time pleasantly until the evening train bore us
Brunswickwards. We hope soon to welcome Princeton to New-Brunswick
for the third game, and best them. Their cheer, sounding as if they meant to
explode, but for a fortunate escape of air, followed by a grateful yell at the
deliverance of such a catastrophe, still sounds in our ears as we thank them for
their hospitality. If we must be beaten we are glad to have such conquerors.

1869 RUTGERS FOOTBALL TEAM:

Captain William James Leggett '72: Reformed Church Pastor, President of the Board of Superintendents of the New Brunswick Reformed Church

Frederick Ernest Allen '73: Methodist Minister

Madison Monroe Ball '73: Teacher

Thomas W. Clemons '72

George Riley Dixson '73: Teacher, Member of Pennsylvania Legislature

Ezra Doane DeLameter '71: Lawyer

Stephen George Gano '71: Civil Engineer

Edward D. Gillmore '72

Daniel Trimble Hawkhurst '73: Bookkeeper

John W. Herbert '72: Lawyer, Rutgers Trustee

William J. Hill '72

Peter "Preston Huyssoon '73: Business Manager

George Hall Large '72: Lawyer, 1888 President New Jersey Senate

Winfield S. Lasher '71

Abram Irving Martine '73: Reformed Church Pastor

George Edger Pace '71: New Jersey Assemblyman

Charles L. Pruyn '71

Claudius Rockefeller '73: Lawyer

Charles Henry Steele '72: Physician

George H. Stevens '72

Jacob Outcalt Van Fleet '73: Reformed Church Pastor

John Alfred Van Nest '72: Reformed Church Pastor

Douwe Ditmars (D.D.) Williamson '70: Architect, Superintendent of Construction of the U.S Treasury Department

Charles Seymour Wright '73: Reformed Church Pastor, U.S. Navy Captain

John Henry Wykoff '71: Presbyterian Missionary in India

1869 PRINCETON FOOTBALL TEAM:

Captain William Stryker Gummere '70: Lawyer, Associate Justice NJ Supreme Court

Charles Scudder Barrett '71: Presbyterian Minister

George S. Billmeyer '71: President of his father's manufacturing company

Homer Davenport Boughner '71: Engineer

William Frazier Henley Buck: '70: Businessman

Francis Clayton Burt '71: Finance, Poet

William Cox Chambers '71: Teacher

Charles Winter Darst '71: Businessman

Chauncey Mitchell Field '71: Physician

William Wetmore Flagler '71: Finance

William Bynum Glenn '70: Lawyer

James Winthrop Hageman '72: Presbyterian Minister

Charles Seth Lane '72: Banker

William Preston Lane '72: Lawyer, Lieutenant Colonel in Maryland National Guard

George Williamson Mann '72: Assaying, Mining

Jacob Edwin Michael '71: Physician

David Mixsell '71: Lawyer

Lee Hampton Nissley '70: Banker

Hughes Oliphant '70: Engineer, Business Executive

Charles Joel Parker '70: Lawyer, Banker

Jerome Edward Sharp '70: Businessman

Alexander Van Rensselaer '71: Director, Drexel Institute

Joel Green Weir '71: Lawyer

Thomas Sears Young '71: Businessman